Y, JUNE 22, 1863.

T WINCHESTER.

'ositions of the Union Forces.

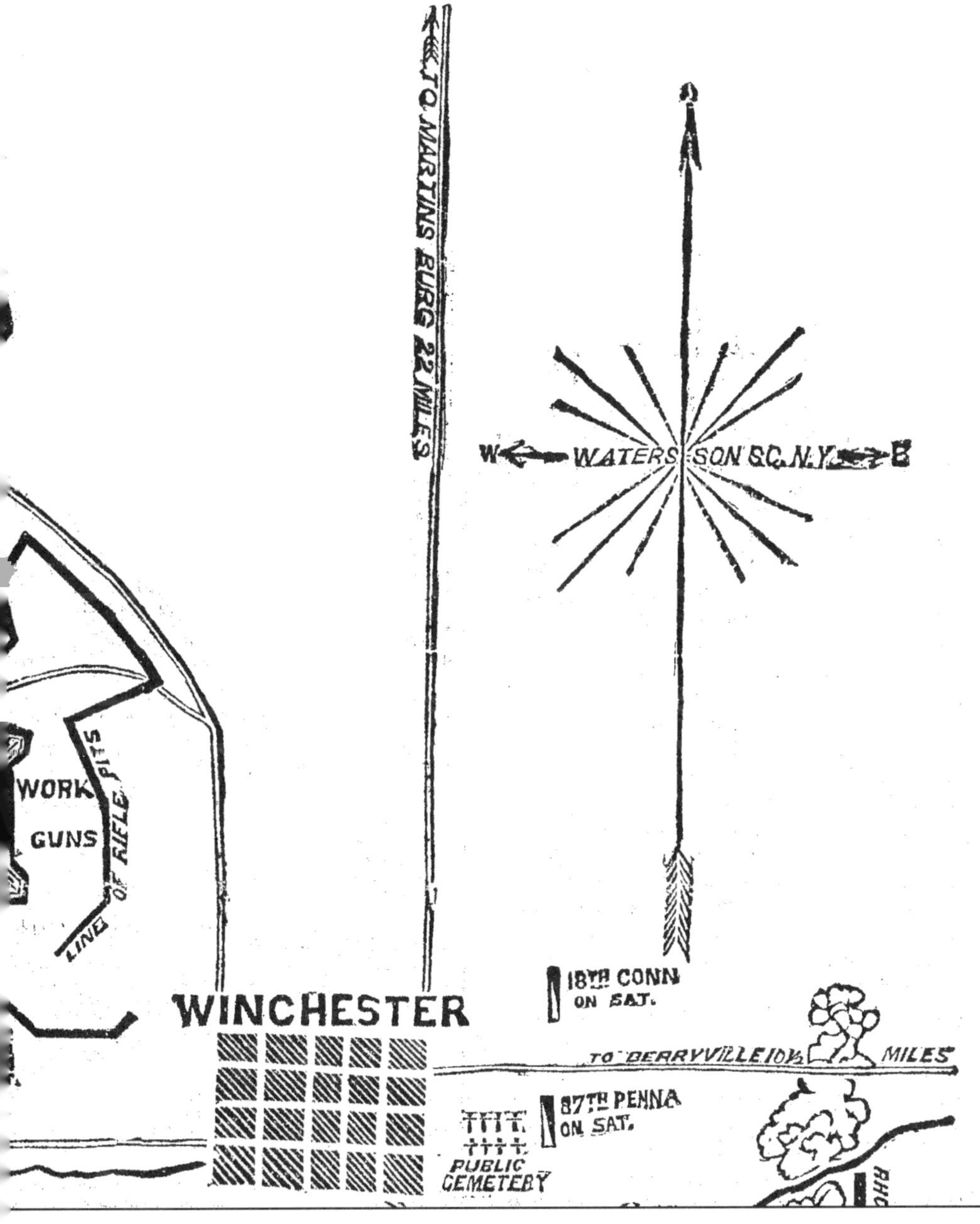

PLAGUED BY WAR:

Winchester, Virginia, During the Civil War

By

Jonathan A. Noyalas

Gauley Mount Press, 313 Lounsbury Court, NE, Leesburg, VA
20176

Published by Gauley Mount Press, 313 Lounsbury Court, NE, Leesburg, VA 20176

ISBN: 0-9628218-9-6

Library of Congress No. 2003311082

Printed in the United States of America

PLAGUED BY WAR:

WINCHESTER, VIRGINIA

DURING THE CIVIL WAR

The Shenandoah Valley

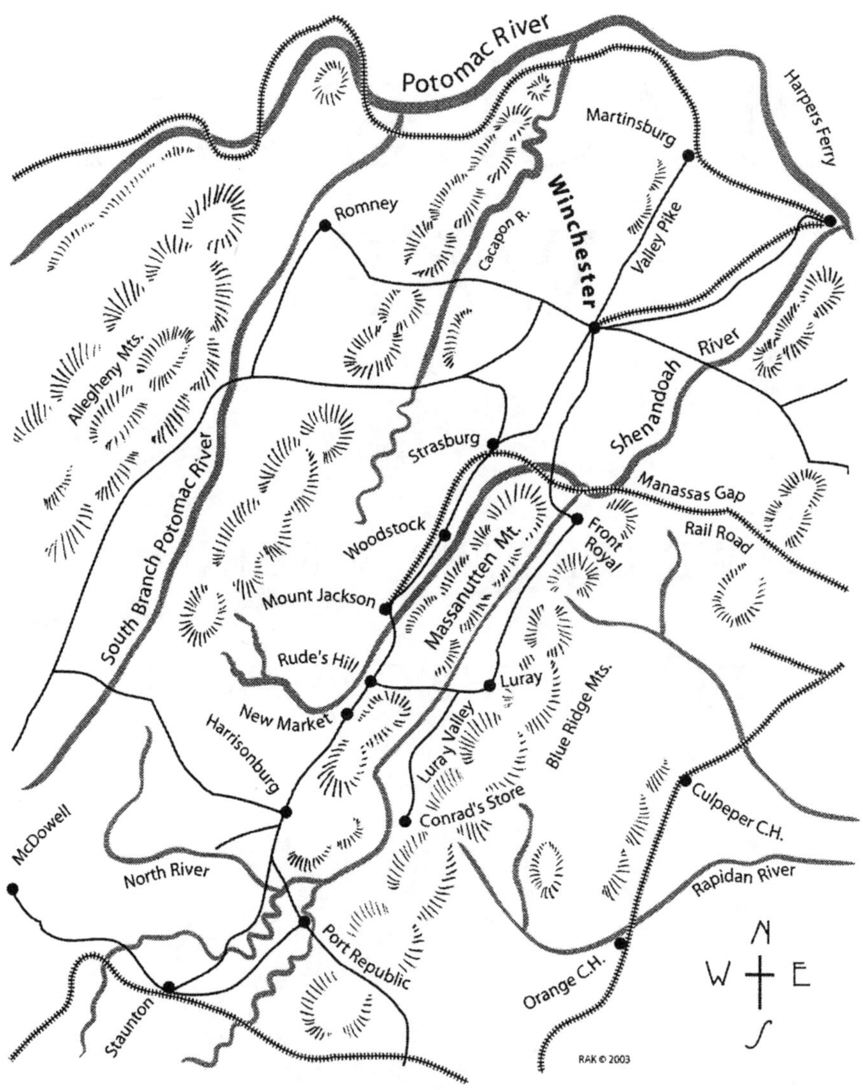

Dedication

This book is dedicated to my mother and father, Arlene and Robert, for their devoted love and support.

Acknowledgements

Any book project would take an author an indefinite amount of time to complete without the help of others. I am indebted to the following individuals for their help and guidance on this project – the photographs division at the Alabama Department of Archives and History for the use of the Richard Ewell photograph; Glenda Brown and the Jasper County Public Library, Jasper County, Indiana, for use of the Robert Milroy Photograph; Dr. Brandon H. Beck, my mentor and holder of the Hugh and Virginia McCormick Chair in Civil War History at Shenandoah University for his guidance, support in all of my historical endeavors, and reading of the manuscript; William C. Davis, director of the Virginia Civil War studies at Virginia Tech for his advice; Roger U. Delauter for clearing up some confusion about the Winchester Militia; Rebecca Ebert and the staff at the Handley Regional Library Archives who helped me gain access to thousands of pages of manuscripts and a number of photographs that appear in this book; Brandy Helmick, a fine historian and the love of my life who helped me with research and listened to revised chapters over and over again; Dr. James I. Robertson, Jr., my graduate mentor at Virginia Tech for his advice, and the interlibrary loan staff at Shenandoah University for their invaluable assistance in locating some much needed material.

Preface

Situated in Virginia's Lower Shenandoah Valley, Winchester thrived as a business community prior to the American Civil War. All of the area's major roads and railroads converged on the town, and the same strategic commercial location that made Winchester thrive also led to its wartime demise.

The town changed hands more times than any other during the American Civil War. The number seventy-two is usually given. Throughout the War, armies of blue and gray came and went about seventy-plus times but the townspeople remained and endured.

Winchester's civilians, especially the women, were as devoted to the Confederacy as any other group in the South. Faced with hardship and harsh treatment by the Union Army, the civilians went about their daily lives and held to their personal ideals. These were strong personalities that did not despair under Union military pressure. Even when some were exiled, they remained light-hearted and devoted to the War for Southern Independence and these civilians picked up the pieces time and again after the armies marched on. Sympathetic women cared for convalescing soldiers on both sides, long after the armies departed.

Plagued by War: Winchester, Virginia, and the Civil War, is a history of military operations in the area coupled with civilian experiences throughout numerous occupations. This study is primarily concerned with the civilian experience of occupation and therefore much of the book is based on the diaries of Winchester's wartime population. Their words paint a clear picture of the

Preface

hardships endured by civilians during this unfortunate period of our history. This work serves as a testimony to the unsung civilian heroes of Winchester who endured war and cared for the wounded men of both blue and gray.

Jonathan A. Noyalas

Blacksburg, Virginia

September 2002

Introduction

The publication of Jonathan Noyalas' *Plagued by War: Winchester, Virginia, and the Civil War* is a signal event in the historiography of the Civil War in the Shenandoah Valley.

Typical in many ways of most Virginia towns, Winchester stood out in 1861 as the county seat of the northernmost secessionist county in the Old Dominion, Frederick County. Noyalas explains the course of secession in Winchester and then demonstrates how Winchester's commanding position in the Lower Shenandoah Valley opened it to the "plague of war".

The town and county witnessed six major engagements and innumerable raids, skirmishes, and actions. The two Battles of Kernstown, the three Battles of Winchester, and the Battle of Cedar Creek each resulted from important strategic decisions and each had important consequences.

First Kernstown (March 23, 1862) began Jackson's Valley Campaign. First Winchester (May 25, 1862) sealed the strategic success of that campaign. Second Winchester (June 14 – 15, 1863) opened the Army of Northern Virginia's invasion of Pennsylvania. The Second Battle of Kernstown (July 24, 1864) was a Confederate victory that ironically set the stage for the defeat of Confederate strategy in the Valley at Third Winchester (September 19, 1864) and the virtual end of any Confederate presence in the Valley at the Battle of Cedar Creek (October 19, 1864). Cedar Creek and Winchester are contiguous; Sheridan began his famous ride to save his army at Cedar Creek at the Logan House in Winchester.

Introduction

The inhabitants of Civil War Winchester included an unusually large number of careful diarists. The archive collection of the Handley Regional Library in Winchester has a rich collection of those works. Noyalas draws on their accounts not only as a mirror of battles but as a window into the life of a town engulfed by war. The author also firmly establishes the battles and leaders within the context of the citizens' lives.

Much of Civil War Winchester remains today. Readers will find in the final section of this book a comprehensive, easy to follow guided tour of Civil War Winchester, containing much information published for the first time.

Jonathan Noyalas earned his BA in history at Shenandoah University in 2001, studying at the McCormick Civil War Institute. The author has completed his graduate studies at Virginia Tech.

His first book is an auspicious beginning of an historian's career. He writes within the oldest and best tradition of American historiography, writing for the general reader, but also for historians of the Civil War in Virginia.

Brandon H. Beck, Ph.D.

Director, McCormick Civil War Institute

Shenandoah University, Winchester, Virginia

October 2002

CONTENTS

The streets of Winchester bustled with activity on October 17, 1859, as men of the 31st Virginia Militia assembled in the streets at the orders of their company commanders. Winchester's streets were not the scenes of a joyous parade; this was a glimpse of the looming war that awaited the town's citizens. The men of the 31st had been summoned to quell violence at Harpers Ferry. Shocked, the militia and townspeople only knew that a fanatical band of abolitionists were attempting to capture the Federal armory at Harpers Ferry.

The day prior to the stunning news, October 16, the radical abolitionist John Brown and his band of raiders entered the United States Armory at Harpers Ferry. Brown hoped to seize its huge store of firearms, cause the slaves in nearby areas to revolt, come to his assistance, and help him to create a new nation. The plan, although meticulously designed, failed miserably.

As a contingent of ninety United States Marines, commanded by Colonel Robert E. Lee, and state militia began to converge on Harpers Ferry, the citizens of the once quiet town took matters into their own hands -- shooting at Brown's intruders from any vantage point that provided a clear shot.[1] As the chaotic events at Harpers Ferry unfolded, the 31st Virginia Militia,

---

[1] Stan Cohen, *John Brown: "The Thundering Voice of Jehovah"* (Missoula, Mt.: Pictorial Histories Publishing, 1999), 50. The note is only for the number figure given.

commanded by Winchester resident Colonel Lewis Tilghman Moore was moving to the troubled town via the Winchester & Potomac Railroad.[2]

Three companies of the 31st Virginia Militia were from Winchester; the Marion Rifles, Winchester Rifles, and the Morgan Continental Guard.[3] The Marion Rifles, organized in the late 1850's, was commanded by Captain John H.J. Funk and his fifty-six man company frequently drilled in the past with imitation rifles on the outskirts of Winchester.[4] Now fully armed, these men had the opportunity to employ their untested skills.

Perhaps the most prestigious of the Winchester companies was the Morgan Continental Guard. This company, organized in the summer of 1855, was named in honor of the local Revolutionary War hero, General Daniel Morgan.[5] The men wore Revolutionary War style uniforms -- blue cloth coats, buckskin breeches, and three-cornered hats. As was customary in most militia units of the period, members had to provide the costly uniforms for themselves.[6] This was a financial obligation that

---

[2] Roger U. Delauter, Jr. *Winchester in the Civil War* (Lynchburg, Va.: H.E. Howard, 1992), 2. The militia was en route on October 17.

[3] The Morgan Continental Guard is also referred to as the Continental Morgan Guard on occasion. There seems to be some dispute and the name is equally applied throughout written material. Roger U. Delauter in *Winchester in the Civil War*, refers to them as the Morgan Continental Guard; the converse is noted in Lee A. Wallace, Jr. *5th Virginia Infantry* (Lynchburg, Va.: H.E. Howard, 1988).

[4] Wallace, 8.

[5] Wallace, 9.

[6] It is important to mention that many militia members in units throughout the country had to provide the funds for their own uniforms.

many members could not meet. In 1857 Winchester's women had recognized the militia volunteers' financial strains and held a benefit fair to raise money for the purchase of the elaborate uniforms.[7]

Winchester's women supported the militia units in other ways. As a further example, they awarded the Marion Rifles a silk United States flag on Independence Day of that fateful year, 1859.[8]

George Washington Kurtz wearing the uniform of the Morgan Continental Guard. The militia company was named in honor of Winchester's Revolutionary War hero General Daniel Morgan, famous for his victory at the Battle of Cowpens, South Carolina, in 1781. (Winchester - Frederick County Historical Society).

---

[7] Wallace, 10. The fair was held on April 3, 1857. The Winchester women raised enough funds to provide uniforms for fifteen members of the company.
[8] Ibid., 8. On Independence Day, 1859 in front of the Court House the women presented the men with the new flag.

The train carried Moore and his militia on the Winchester and Potomac Railroad as far as Halltown. There they left the cars and marched the remaining four miles to Harpers Ferry. Once they arrived, the primary responsibility assigned to the militia was the guarding of the vital Baltimore and Ohio Railroad trestle. Fortunately, the men of the 31st Virginia Militia did not have to engage John Brown's raiders.

A contingent of United States Marines under the command of Colonel Robert E. Lee arrived late during the night of October 17, to find Brown's raiders confined in a small fire engine house in the town. During the Nat Turner Rebellion in 1831, Lee was stationed at Fort Monroe and he knew the high potential for bloodshed implicit in a slave rebellion.[9] In a three-minute fight the next morning, twenty-seven marines commanded by First Lieutenant Israel Greene stormed "John Brown's Fort" and killed or captured the raiders and captured Brown.[10] Brown was taken to Charles Town, Virginia, and put on trial for murder, treason against the Commonwealth of Virginia, and attempting to arm slaves.[11] Brown's actions at Harpers Ferry were vehemently attacked by most Southerners, but a majority of radical Northern abolitionists sympathized with him.

---

[9] Douglas Southall Freeman, *R.E. Lee* (New York: Charles Scribner's Sons, 1934), 1:394.

[10] Cohen, 53.

[11] Ibid., 79 Patricia L. Faust, ed., *Historical Times Illustrated Encyclopedia Of The Civil War* (New York: Harper Perennial, 1991), 83.

Brown's popularity among violent abolitionists heightened the possibility that an attempt might be made to free him.

Virginia's governor, Henry Wise, recognized this threat and ordered state troops to Charles Town to prevent such a disaster. On October 31, 1859, the men of the Morgan Continental Guard boarded a train and headed for Charles Town to prevent any attempt to free Brown and the others who were captured.[12]

In a strange twist of fate the first man to die in Brown's raid was a free black from Winchester, Heyward Shepherd. Shepherd worked at the Harpers Ferry depot as a baggage handler. He was shot in the back by one of the raiders when he refused to comply with their order for him to halt. Mortally wounded, he lingered for approximately twelve hours before dying. This act of cruelty enraged the citizens of Winchester and his lifeless body was buried with military honors in a "Black" cemetery south of Winchester.[13] Shepherd left behind a wife and eight children for whom the citizens of Winchester established a relief fund.

Heyward Shepherd and Moore's militia were not Winchester's only connections with the Harpers Ferry raid. Several students from the Winchester Medical College were curious about the event and decided to trek to Harpers Ferry. As the students approached the town they found the slain body of one

---

[12] There is no record that mentions any of the other Winchester militia companies headed to Charles Town for that purpose. Cadets from the Virginia Military Institute and other militia units from all over the state were present as well.

[13] Delauter, 4.

of Brown's raiders, later discovered to be the remains of Brown's son, Watson. The students took the corpse back to the college to be used for dissection and study. This act of disrespect embedded itself in the minds of stern abolitionists who later became Union soldiers. The college paid severely for this act of human disrespect in the ensuing war.[14]

Judge Richard Parker, a native of Winchester, presided over Brown's State treason trial. Brown was found guilty of treason against Virginia and hanged on December 2, 1859. Sent to Charles Town to guard the execution site, the Morgan Continental Guard returned to Winchester three days after the execution.

The emotional and political gaps between North and South widened after Brown's raid, and became unbridgeable after the election of Abraham Lincoln in November 1860. Between the raid and the election, however, Winchester returned to something resembling normality.

The census of 1860 for Winchester lists 4,403 inhabitants, including 3,040 whites, 655 freedmen, and 708 slaves.[15] The population of Frederick County, including slaves, exceeded 14,000.[16] There were 2,317 votes cast in Winchester and Frederick County in the 1860 presidential election, 1,315 of which were for

---

[14] The event will be discussed further in the book, but the college was burned by Union soldiers in the Spring of 1862.

[15] Garland R. Quarles. *Occupied Winchester: 1861 – 1865* (Winchester, Va.: Winchester-Frederick County Historical Society, 1991), 2.

[16] Ibid., 2.

the southern Democrat, John C. Breckinridge. Still, most Winchester voters remained largely opposed to secession.[17]

By 1860 the community was flourishing as a major center of business activity in the Lower Shenandoah Valley. Most of the regions major roads passed through the town, the most important of which was the paved Valley Pike. The Pike ran north to south for nearly 100 miles from Winchester south to Staunton. Other major roads converged on the town as well. From the east came Berryville Pike while Millwood Pike came from the southeast, the Martinsburg Pike from the north, and the Northwestern Pike from the west. The Winchester and Potomac Railroad provided a route to Harpers Ferry, and from here routes east and west via its junction with the Baltimore and Ohio Railroad. The strategic location of Winchester promoted its economic prominence and that location brought about its wartime problems.

On December 20, 1860, South Carolina seceded from the Union and six other Deep South states followed soon thereafter. Because of the compromises inspired by Henry Clay, Virginia remained loyal to the Union -- even with the secession of seven Deep South states. Virginia, however, was in a precarious situation; it was going to become a border state if it did not secede, but its social, economic, and political ties linked the Old Dominion closely to the agricultural South. With considerable pressure placed on Virginia by its already seceded brethren, a secession

---

[17] Delauter, 5.

convention was called on February 13, 1861, to meet in Richmond. It was at this convention that the fate of Virginia – and arguably the nation – hung in the balance.

Mass meetings were held throughout all Virginia to discuss the issue of secession and provide a slate of candidates to be sent to the secession convention to be held in Richmond. A special election was held on February 4, 1861, and two representatives were to be selected from Winchester, the county seat of Frederick County.

On January 23, 1861, a mass meeting was held in town to nominate candidates for the election.[18] Robert Conrad and James Marshall were the two candidates chosen for their strong Union sentiment and the secession candidates were F.W.M. Holliday and Peyton Clark.[19] Given his German and Scotch-Irish background, Holliday was an unlikely advocate of secession.[20]

Winchester's citizens understood the gravity of the situation, knowing Virginia would become a battleground however the secession question was decided. Because the lower South already had seceded, Virginia, regardless of its affiliation, would

---

[18] Rev. Benjamin F. Brooke. "Journal, Sept. 1837 – Dec. 25, 1863," 165 WFCHS – Brooke Collection, Archives Room, Handley Regional Library, Winchester, Va. In his journal entry for January 23, 1861 he writes the following: "All day at the mass meeting held to elect Union candidates to the Virginia Convention to be held in February…"

[19] Quarles, 4.

[20] James Tice Moore, "Of Cavaliers and Yankees Frederick W.M. Holliday and the Sectional Crisis 1845 - 1861" *The Virginia Magazine of History and Biography* (July 1991), 353. Those of German and Scotch Irish background were not traditionally advocates of secession.

be a main thoroughfare for troops entering the South or heading north. Therefore battle on Virginia soil was imminent.

Reverend Benjamin F. Brooke of the Market Street Methodist Church preached to his congregation on the Sunday morning, prior to the election, saying: "Young men, take off your badges of Disunion, and rather put on mourning – mourning for your Mother… But there is one hope left – and that last hope is the mediation of Virginia".[21]

There is no doubt Reverend Brooke expressed the sentiment of many of Winchester's citizens during the time between secession and the firing on Fort Sumter. Unionist candidates Conrad and Marshall defeated secessionists Holliday and Clark for seats at the secession convention.[22] The people were ardently opposed to secession at the time and in favor of a peaceful resolution. Many of Winchester's residents were German, English, Scottish, or Irish Quakers who traditionally owned no slaves. Moreover, by the 1830's the institution of slavery decreased in economic importance.[23] Even in Frederick County, where the number of slaves was far greater, the economy did not depend on the institution as it did in the counties east of the Blue Ridge.

---

[21] Brooke, journal entry for February 3, 1861.

[22] While there is a substantial amount of information on Robert Conrad, the information on James Marshall is sparse. Prior to the Civil War he was an attorney in Winchester, but beyond this the historical record on Marshall is quite sketchy. The information about him being an attorney is contained in: J.E. Norris, *History of the Lower Shenandoah Valley Counties of Frederick, Berkeley, Jefferson, and Clarke* (Chicago: A. Warner and Co., 1890), 194.

[23] Moore, 356.

Perhaps one reason for the decline in the importance of slavery was the migration of non-slaveholding individuals from Ohio and Pennsylvania into the Shenandoah Valley.[24] Additionally slavery was not to become a reason for secession in Winchester after the firing on Fort Sumter.

The two men elected to the convention went to Richmond to help decide the fate of the state. Conrad, although ardently opposed to what he regarded as the fanaticism of Abraham Lincoln and the Republican Party, felt strongly that the Union should be preserved – unless the cost of loyalty was state sovereignty.[25] Conrad also acted as the chairman of the Committee on Federal Relations. As chairman of the committee, Conrad did everything in his power to pursue a proper and peaceful solution to the secession crisis that threatened the nation's existence.

In the first vote of the convention on the fourth of April, secession was defeated by a margin of eighty-eight to forty-five votes.[26] In the meantime, however, sentiment in Winchester had slowly changed. Two days after the vote a meeting was held in front of the courthouse where several fiery orators preached for secession. Several months prior to this many of these same men preached union.[27] There is no simple explanation for why these

---

[24] John W. Wayland, *Twenty-Five Chapters on the Shenandoah Valley: To which is Appended a Concise History of the Civil War in the Valley* (Harrisonburg, Va.: C.J. Carrier Co. 1976), 83.
[25] David F. Riggs, "Robert Young Conrad and the Ordeal of Secession", *Virginia Magazine of History and Biography* (July 1978), 259-60.
[26] Delauter, 7.
[27] Brooke, journal entry for April 6, 1861.

men changed their sentiment toward secession. Perhaps some changed their minds when they learned of the letter sent on April 6, by President Lincoln to Governor Francis Pickens of South Carolina informing the governor that the Federal government was going to supply Fort Sumter. It is possible that these former anti-secessionists saw the attempt to supply Fort Sumter as an infringement on state sovereignty in South Carolina, and decided if it could happen in South Carolina it could happen in Virginia. Still, some people remained opposed to secession in Winchester. Many of these individuals, however, decided to remain loyal to Virginia regardless of the circumstances. Reverend Brooke expressed this sentiment on the day of the court house speeches when he wrote: "… heard some secession speeches at the Court House, now believe Virginia will cut her own throat – I shall be loyal to her in any case."[28]

On April 12, 1861, only six days after the meeting at the courthouse, the first shots of war echoed in Charleston Harbor. Now, it was the acts of the Federal Government that determined Virginia's course to secession. Most Virginians viewed President Lincoln's ill-fated attempt to supply Fort Sumter and his call for 75,000 volunteers to suppress the "rebellion" after Sumter surrendered to be a declaration of war against the South. On April 17, Virginia's Secession Convention passed the ordinance of secession in a second vote by eighty-eight votes to fifty-five.

---

[28] Ibid.

Again Conrad and Marshall voted against secession. Conrad, however, made it known that he would stand firmly by his state. Robert Conrad, once a staunch supporter of the Union sent five of his sons into the service of the Confederate States and he later denounced both the legitimacy and actions of the United States Government.[29]

The scenes from October 1859, when the streets of Winchester bulged with militia troops would be repeated many times over in the ensuing war. For Winchester, the experience of John Brown's raid was only a mild preview as Winchester gained military significance as the war developed. The magnitude of its importance grew daily as the Civil War progressed. The once quiet, prosperous Virginia town became a key to victory for both sides as the crucial importance of the Shenandoah Valley became recognized by Union and Confederate military planners. As the stage was prepared for the terrible conflict, this once peaceful community found itself at the epicenter of a calamity.

---

[29] Quarles, 4. It should be mentioned here that both Conrad and Marshall ran for the Virginia legislature in 1861, however, they were beaten by a substantial margin. It was after this time that Conrad changed his sentiment.

With the destruction of the political compromises of the past decades, the reality of war emerged. Simultaneously with secession, Governor John Letcher ordered the seizure of the Federal armory at Harpers Ferry and less than twenty-four hours later militia units streamed into Winchester.[30] These men soon boarded trains on the Winchester and Potomac Railroad for the short trip to the armory. Due to the close proximity of the town, the Winchester companies were among the first to reach the arsenal on the evening of April 18.[31]

Governor Letcher's orders were simple -- occupy the armory and collect anything of military use. The United States Army commander at the Harpers Ferry Armory, First Lieutenant Roger Jones, burned the buildings, destroying many of the weapons the Confederacy needed before the force of 600 Rebel militia arrived. The Virginia militia force was commanded by a former U.S. Army artillery officer and Virginia Military Institute professor -- Thomas Jonathan Jackson, who was soon to become "Stonewall" after the First Battle of Manassas.[32] He salvaged numerous items including rifles, rifled muskets, and stock blanks.[33]

---

[30] Archie P. McDonald, ed., *"To Live and Die in Dixie": How the South Formed a Nation* (Murfreesboro: Southern Heritage Press, 1999), 94; Delauter, 8.
[31] James I. Robertson Jr. *The Stonewall Brigade* (Baton Rouge: Louisiana State University Press, 1991), 5.
[32] William B. Edwards, "Guns for the South" *Confederate Veteran* (Vol. 1, 2001), 8.
[33] Ibid., 9.

Over the course of the next several weeks, soldiers moved through Winchester *en route* to Harpers Ferry, which had become a mustering post for men entering into Confederate service. Colonel Jackson, who remained in command at Harpers Ferry, first rode through the streets of Winchester on April 29, 1861.[34]

Winchester's militia companies returned to familiar ground at Harpers Ferry. This time, however, the men were there to be drilled and organized into an effective fighting unit in Virginia's Army. Colonel Jackson drew on his West Point education, Mexican War service, and experience as a teacher at the Virginia Military Institute to shape these men into soldiers through grueling hours of both drill and guard duty.

The Winchester militia companies were mustered into service and received new designations – the Winchester Rifles became Co. I, 2nd Regiment Virginia Infantry, the Marion Rifles became Co. A, 5th Regiment Virginia Infantry, and the Morgan Continental Guards became Co. K, 5th Regiment Virginia Infantry. Lewis Tilghman Moore, previously the colonel of the 31st Virginia Militia became a lieutenant colonel in the 4th Regiment Virginia Infantry.

Perhaps one of the most noted anecdotes of the early part of the war concerns Jackson and the trains on the Baltimore and Ohio Railroad. The story, related post-war by John D. Imboden, was that Jackson, annoyed at the noise created by trains coming in and

---

[34] James I. Robertson, Jr., *Stonewall Jackson: The Man, The Soldier, The Legend* (New York: Macmillan, 1997), 221.

out of Harpers Ferry caused him to block the tracks running east at Point of Rocks and then close the other line at Martinsburg.[35]

Trapping many separate trains, both locomotives and rolling stock, between his barricades, Jackson captured trains needed so badly by the Confederacy. Jackson's biographer, Dr. James I. Robertson, Jr. has dismissed this story as fiction. There would have been numerous complications had Jackson actually done this.[36]

On May 24, Jackson turned over his command at Harpers Ferry to Major General Joseph E. Johnston.[37] Johnston, a West Point contemporary of Robert E. Lee, assessed the position at Harpers Ferry and determined it was neither the place to organize an army nor the point from which to defend the Shenandoah Valley. Johnston possessed extensive engineering experience and quickly found that the town was indefensible. He believed the defensive key to the Shenandoah Valley was Winchester.[38] Aware of the strategic importance of Winchester, Johnston also knew, courtesy of a report in a Hagerstown, Maryland newspaper, that somewhere north of town was a Union force of 18,000 under

---

[35] John D. Imboden is noted for his excellent service as a cavalry officer, however, in 1861 he commanded the Staunton Artillery. It was not until 1862 that he organized his 1st Partisan Rangers.

[36] Robertson, *Stonewall Jackson: The Man, The Soldier, The Legend*, 229. On this page the last two paragraphs discount Imboden's anecdote.

[37] Joseph E. Johnston's rank at this time can be confusing to some. After offering his service to Virginia in late April 1861, Johnston was made a major general, however, on May 14, 1861, he was commissioned a brigadier general in the Confederate Army.

[38] Delauter, 9.

command of Major General Robert Patterson, an elderly Federal officer who served in the War of 1812.[39] Patterson was discharged from the service on July 27, 1861, due to his failure to contain Johnston. Johnston immediately sent word to Richmond requesting permission to withdraw his command to Winchester.[40]

While awaiting orders, Johnston prepared for the move to Winchester. He blocked most of the roads along the Potomac River and loaded his army's wagons in anticipation of Richmond's approval. After several weeks, on June 13, Adjutant General Samuel Cooper authorized Johnston to withdraw when the enemy threatened his position at Harpers Ferry.[41]

Moments after Johnston read Cooper's dispatch he ordered the evacuation of the post at Harpers Ferry and destroyed everything that could not be taken to Winchester.[42] Johnston's "Army of the Shenandoah" arrived at Bunker Hill on June 16, and the following day was within four miles of Winchester. General

---

[39] Craig L. Symonds, *Joseph E. Johnston: A Civil War Biography* (New York: W.W. Norton & Company, 1992), 107.

[40] General Johnston, while in command of the post did not have the liberty withdraw under his own volition. He had to obtain orders first that allowed him to withdraw when practicable.

[41] Robertson. *Stonewall Jackson: The Man, The Soldier, The Legend,* 243. The reason that Johnston felt threatened was that he knew that there was a Federal force in the vicinity of his position and that he was unable to defend himself properly at Harper's Ferry. Winchester provided him with the ability to protect his command and fortify it as well with earthworks, etc.

[42] Ibid, 243.

Johnston went directly to the town and set up headquarters at the Taylor Hotel while his men camped on the outskirts of the city.[43]

After conferring with his chief engineer, Major William Henry Chase Whiting, Johnston ordered the construction of defensive works north of town. One site chosen was Benjamin Stine's farm; it commanded the approach to Winchester on the Martinsburg Pike from which direction Patterson's force was expected. The construction of the fort was first supervised by a Lieutenant Collier -- for whom the fort was later named.[44] Initially, the laborers came from militia units sent to Winchester and after Jackson's first action at the Battle of Falling Waters on July 2, 1861, forty-five prisoners of war were included in the working parties building Fort Collier.[45] The skirmish at Falling Waters was small by Civil War standards with Jackson's force of about 350 men battling Brigadier General John J. Abercrombie's

---

[43] Delauter, 10. There seems to be a controversy as to where Johnston had his headquarters. There is some written material that suggests his headquarters was not in the town, however, the evidence strongly leans toward that notion. While it is mentioned that Confederate soldiers under Johnston's command did not arrive near Winchester until the 17th there is also evidence that Confederate soldiers were present in Winchester in the days prior to this. Reverend Brooke in his journal for June 14, 1861, pens the following: "Winchester full of soldiers – making a military post of it – so it becomes a center of war."

[44] It is believed that the soldiers who constructed Fort Collier were Alabama soldiers. Only one regiment of Alabama soldiers, the 4th, was in Winchester during the time of its construction, they were part of Brigadier General Barnard Bee's brigade. The historical record on Lieutenant Collier is quite unclear. Historians who have researched Fort Collier have been unable to turn up a first name for the lieutenant.

[45] Quarles, 59. The Battle of Falling Waters occurred on July 2, 1861, and was only a skirmish by later standards of the war. The battle site is located just north of Winchester in present day West Virginia.

3,000-man brigade.   After about half an hour the heavily outnumbered Confederates withdrew to end the small battle.[46]

The work on the fortifications north of town took several months to complete and continued well after the departure of Johnston's command for Manassas on July 18.   One of Winchester's inquisitive residents, Harriet Griffith, who married a member of Major General Philip Sheridan's staff after the war, visited the fort in late August and wrote:

> I have this day visited the breastworks or fortifications out on the Martinsburg Pike with Father and Johnnie. Was exceedingly interested. First work of the kind I'd ever seen. The first time I was ever so near a cannon. I looked into them. The cannon balls weigh 42 pounds each. There were four cannons planted and much ammunition there. A great many men were working [and I] saw the magazines. They have several rifle ports which seem so secure. I have read of them, but have never seen them. They had several masked batteries. It seems real strong and well built. There is a high embankment of sand bags, barrels, and brush covered with dirt, part sodded over. They intend to sod it with a big ditch on the lower side. They have completely surrounded Stine's House which is now occupied by soldiers, some of whom were working there, some cooking, some washing, some on guard, and some lounging, and some sleeping… Surely it is something to be remembered, but I hope it will never be used.[47]

---

[46] Robertson, *Stonewall Jackson: The Man, The Soldier, The Legend,* 249-50.

[47] Harriet H. Griffith Diary. 208 WFCHS – Allan Tischler Collection, Archives Room, Handley Regional Library. Diary entry is for August 21, 1861. The guns in place were those captured at Harpers Ferry in the spring of 1861.

While at Winchester, Johnston also contended with a problem soon to become all too familiar to generals on both sides: measles. The epidemic broke out in late June and afflicted large numbers of soldiers. Most of Johnston's men came from rural families living in relative isolation and never contracted measles to gain immunity during childhood. As a result, large numbers of young men in both armies caught measles at the same time.

Major General Joseph E. Johnston was the first commander of the post at Winchester. Johnston took command of the Valley Army on May 24, 1861 and made the decision to move his command to Winchester. Johnston commanded the army when it marched out of Winchester in July headed for the first major land engagement at Manassas Junction. On August 31, 1861 Johnston was commissioned a full general. During the Battle of Seven Pines, May 31, 1862, Johnston was wounded and did not return to the army until November of that year. After his return to the army he commanded the Department of the West and after General Braxton Bragg's debacle at Chattanooga in late 1863 commanded the Army of Tennessee Army of Tennessee once again. Johnston surrendered his command to Sherman on April 26, 1865. He died in 1891. (Winchester – Frederick County Historical Society)

Mortality rates from complications such as pneumonia reached as high as twenty-five percent in some units. Hotels, churches, and warehouses were converted into hospitals to house and treat the ill soldiers. Reverend Brooke, still doing his part for the Confederate cause, allowed the Market Street Methodist Church to be used as a hospital and on June 22, Brooke sold his camp meeting tent to a group of soldiers from Alabama.[48]

The terrible sight of young soldiers dying from disease paled in comparison to the first horrifying images of dead and wounded from battle. Jackson's skirmish at Falling Waters brought the first of hundreds of casualties to Winchester. Early in the war the medical services of both armies used buildings located near the fighting as hospitals and heart-rending scenes were repeated in Winchester's larger buildings time and again during the war.

Orders reached Johnston early on the morning of July 18, to move to the aid of Brigadier General P.G.T. Beauregard at Manassas.[49] Johnston marched his army out of Winchester at approximately 1 p.m. that afternoon. Moving behind a screen of Confederate cavalry that blinded Union General Patterson to its intentions, the Army of the Shenandoah, led by Jackson's brigade,

---

[48] Brooke, journal, entries for June 16 & 22, 1861. It is unclear if Brooke sold his tent to the soldiers to use as a hospital but it identifies the need for tents and a lack of them in the Army of the Shenandoah.

[49] P.G.T. Beauregard held the rank of brigadier general at the time the order was sent to Johnston. He would be promoted to full general in the Confederate Army on July 21, 1861.

marched southeast on the Millwood Pike for Piedmont Station on the Manassas Gap Railroad. After a twenty-three mile march, Johnston's men crammed themselves into boxcars for the remaining thirty-four miles to Manassas Junction. In the ensuing battle at Manassas, Jackson's brigade turned the tide of battle and earned Jackson his eternal sobriquet of "Stonewall" after General Barnard Bee shouted: "look at Jackson… there he stands like a stone wall! Rally behind the Virginians!"[50]

As Johnston's army departed Winchester that afternoon emotions in the town ran high as many in his command were natives of Winchester. Those that remained were mostly woman, children, old men, and clergy and many feared for the men who were marching off to unknown fates.

Kate Sperry of Winchester was eighteen years old in 1861 and her father, Warden Warren Sperry, answered Virginia's call when he enlisted as a member of the 2nd Virginia Infantry.[51] She epitomized the plight of women in the town as she not only had to contend with rotating occupying forces, but she constantly feared for the safety of a loved one. Kate bade farewell to her father

---

[50] The exact words that General Bee uttered are unknown. The phrase quoted here is taken from: Mary Anna Jackson, *Memoirs of "Stonewall" Jackson* (Dayton, Oh.: Morningside Bookshop, 1976), 179.

[51] Kate Sperry, *Surrender? Never Surrender*, Archives Room, Handley Regional Library. In the diary there is an article regarding a service inspired by her diary, the information about her father comes from that article. Her father's first name was Warden and ought not to be confused with the title of someone in charge of a jail.

during the afternoon on July 18' and from her home at 41 South Loudoun Street, she wrote the following:

> This morning all our army, 25,000 men, rec'd orders to march from here to the Junction to assist Beauregarde [sic] who was having a glorious fight with the Yankees. I never felt as sad in all my life. I went to the door to see them go by.[52]

Only two militia units remained to defend the town.[53] These men grumbled about being called to active service as they believed enough volunteers had been assembled in the state to guard Winchester and complete Fort Collier. Julia Chase, an ardent Unionist in the town, noted: "The Militia are still coming in, and a great many complain bitterly about their being called out, when [there are] so many Volunteers in this State."[54] Once Johnston's army marched away, the town presented the peaceful appearance for the first time in over a month.

The tranquil scene ended abruptly when news of the Confederate victory at Manassas reached the citizens. On the evening of July 23, the price of the South's victory became evident as wagons loaded with wounded soldiers began to arrive in Winchester. [55] Many of the wounded and dead were from the ranks of the families of the town. For a second time in the early

---

[52] Ibid., entry for July 18, 1861.
[53] Robertson, *Stonewall Jackson: The Man, The Soldier, The Legend*, 254.
[54] Julia Chase, Diary, Archives Room, Handley Regional Library, Entry for July 20-21.
[55] Delauter, 12.

days of the war, Winchester's homes, hotels, churches, and warehouses were transformed into hospitals for the wounded.

After the defeat of the Federal Army at Manassas, a lull ensued in combat operations that continued until early November. On the night of November 4, the hero of Manassas, former Colonel and now Major General Thomas Jonathan "Stonewall" Jackson, arrived in Winchester with two of his staff officers, J.T.L. Preston and Alexander "Sandie" Pendleton.[56]   The three men were assigned room number twenty-three in the Taylor Hotel on Loudoun Street.[57]   The next morning numerous citizens came to the hotel to meet "Stonewall", the hero of Manassas.

Jackson was promoted to major general on October 7, and given command of the Valley District of the newly organized Department of Northern Virginia with its headquarters at Winchester.[58]   The new department, now commanded by General Johnston, included two other districts, the Potomac District commanded by General Beauregard, and the Aquia District commanded by Major General Theophilus Holmes.[59]

Confederate troops poured into the Winchester area during the days after Jackson arrived.   The most notable unit was the famed "Stonewall" Brigade, which was comprised of many men

---

[56] Robertson, *Stonewall Jackson: The Man, The Soldier, The Legend*, 284.

[57] Ibid., 284.

[58] John D. Imboden, "Stonewall Jackson in the Shenandoah," *Battles and Leaders of the Civil War*, 4:282.

[59] Theophilus Holmes was promoted to Major General on October 7, 1861, and given command of the district, but in mid – March 1862 he was ordered to the Department of North Carolina.

from the area. Kate Sperry, probably jubilant over the opportunity to see her father, a member of the brigade, wrote: "Well Jackson's Brigade has really started – a good many of them came in town this morning and squads are still coming…"[60]

By mid-November, Jackson established his camps approximately four miles north of Winchester and because he prohibited the men from entering the town, the citizens often visited the camps. Townspeople frequenting the camps visited their loved ones and some curious inhabitants came to learn about artillery and military technology. Kate Sperry, a member of both groups, visited the Rockbridge Artillery's camp on November 19, and recorded her visit: "… went out to see [William Nelson] Pendleton's Battery… showed us pieces taken from the Yanks on the 21st [of] July – also the way in which a cannon is fired off, the loading etc., the difference between canister and grape, bomb shells etc."[61]

Jackson's methods of stern discipline were tested a few weeks after his arrival. In late October, and prior to Jackson's actual arrival in Winchester, a drunken cavalry soldier, James Alexander Miller, struck his captain while under the influence of liquor. Both cavalrymen attended a dinner during which they drank too freely and got into a heated dispute. A court martial later sentenced Miller to death.

---

[60] Sperry, diary entry for November 9, 1861.
[61] Ibid., entry for November 19, 1861.

On Jackson's arrival, a group of citizens sympathetic to Miller's plight asked him to reduce the penalty. "A number of us went to see General Jackson in the poor fellow's behalf," wrote Reverend Brooke. Jackson, in his strict manner, replied to the plea, 'If you don't find discipline in the army, where will you find it?'" Jackson, however, was developing an increasing respect for the inhabitants and they for him. Brooke, a man who no doubt was fond of the General, was disheartened at the remark. Brooke peered at Jackson and noticed that Stonewall had a tear in his eye. Jackson suggested to Brooke that a petition should be sent to President Jefferson Davis on behalf of the condemned soldier. Miller was pardoned by Davis, but the courier delivering Miller's reprieve drank himself into a stupor and failed to arrive before the execution on November 26. "Baptized James Alexander Miller and attended him at his execution… He was shot at 12 in the field at the edge of town." recalled Reverend Brooke.[62]

Within two weeks of his arrival, Jackson moved his headquarters from the Taylor Hotel to Lewis Tilghman Moore's home (located at present day 415 North Braddock Street). Moore, wounded at Manassas, graciously offered his home to Jackson, who gratefully accepted. Jackson adored the home and in a letter to his wife, Mary Anna, on November 16, described its beauty.[63] Jackson was elated to reside in the Moore home as he had been

---

[62] Brooke, journal entry for November 26, 1861. The entire paragraph is constructed from the information presented in this particular journal entry.
[63] Jackson, 209.

disturbed by frequent visitors at the Taylor Hotel. To ensure privacy at the Moore residence, Jackson assigned a twenty-four hour guard at the home, a duty fulfilled by the Liberty Hall Volunteers.[64]

In the early days of December, Jackson planned to move his command northward in an operation designed to destroy the dams of the Chesapeake and Ohio Canal. The canal's main purpose was to transport coal from Cumberland, Maryland, to Washington, D.C., and Baltimore. General Jackson believed the destruction of the canal would retard some war-related industries in the North because coal was a key strategic commodity. The most crucial location along the canal was at Dam No. 5 near Martinsburg. If this section was destroyed, water transportation would be cut off from Washington west to Cumberland, Maryland and beyond. Jackson's first attempt to destroy Dam No. 5 on December 7-8 failed. The Confederate force, commanded by Major Frank Paxton, was unable to dislodge the Union artillery and sharpshooters guarding the dam. A second attempt at breaching it got underway on December 16, and achieved success on December 21, and the troops then returned to Winchester.[65]

By this point in the war, Jackson felt that the situation in Winchester was sufficiently secure for his wife to join him. Mrs. Jackson arrived at the Taylor Hotel late on December 21. As she

---

[64] Robertson, *Stonewall Jackson: The Man, The Soldier, The Legend*, 292. The Liberty Hall Volunteers were a company in the 4th Regiment Virginia Infantry.
[65] Robertson, *The Stonewall Brigade*, 56-7.

proceeded up the stairs of the hotel, Jackson emerged from the darkness, embraced his wife from behind and kissed her. The happy couple then proceeded to the Moore residence. Mary Anna's stay at the Moore home, however, was brief. When the Romney Campaign began on January 1, she moved in with Reverend James Robert Graham and his wife Fanny.[66] Reverend Graham was the minister at the Kent Street Presbyterian Church in Winchester, where Jackson frequently worshipped. When Jackson returned in late January, he boarded with the Grahams, but he utilized the Moore home as his office.

Jackson received welcome reinforcements on Christmas Day with the arrival of 6,000 troops under the command of Brigadier General William W. Loring.[67] As the men braved the bitter cold and waited for the word to make winter camp, Jackson planned for the occupation of Romney, Virginia (later to become West Virginia).

Romney, less than forty miles northwest of Winchester, was strategically positioned adjacent to the vital Baltimore and Ohio Railroad that ran through the South Branch Valley for 100 miles. The occupation of Romney would yield control of the South Branch Valley and from this location, Jackson's force could ensure the safety of Winchester.

---

[66] James Robert Graham, "Some Reminiscences of Stonewall Jackson" *Things and Thoughts*, (Vol. 1, 1901), 123.
[67] Robertson, *The Stonewall Brigade*, 57.

The occupation of Romney placed Jackson between Federal forces west of Staunton and the Union regiments along the Potomac River line to ensure the safety of Winchester. If a Union force gained control of Romney, however, Jackson's position at Winchester would be threatened. Additionally, Union forces had already scoured the countryside around Romney for food and supplies, and with its close proximity to Winchester, Jackson feared the town would meet the same fate.

Jackson, a student of Napoleon's campaigns, was convinced that a winter campaign, unlike sedentary camp life, reduced the spread of disease.[68] He intended to execute the campaign swiftly, but the poor weather conditions hindered his command's mobility. A much needed break in the oppressive weather occurred several days after Christmas and on New Year's Eve the men were ordered to prepare rations and equipment for a march. Speculation spread through the camps about their destination and some correctly guessed Romney was their goal.

After months of careful planning, Jackson initiated his plan to sever the connection between Brigadier General Benjamin F. Kelley's force at Romney and that of Major General Nathaniel P. Banks along the Potomac. Occupying Romney meant security for Winchester and reduced the possibility that Jackson would be attacked in the Shenandoah Valley; Jackson believed that no single Union army would attack his force. Circumstances, however,

---

[68] Douglas Southall Freeman, *Lee's Lieutenants* (New York: Charles Scribner's Sons, 1942), 1:122.

proved that Jackson's worst enemy during the campaign was not anyone in a blue uniform. As they had for Napoleon, harsh winter storms became a limiting factor for Jackson's small army.

In the breaking dawn of a new year, Stonewall Jackson marched his men toward Romney. The first day was unseasonably warm and the men removed their overcoats and placed them into the wagons accompanying the columns. By mid-day, however, the balmy weather vanished and winter returned in full force. Jackson and his men spent the first miserable, frigid night near Pughtown (present day Gainsboro) where the men soon regretted removing their warm clothes and placing them in the wagons, because the wagons were now well behind the column. The men huddled together, shared their inadequate clothing and blankets, and attempted to stay warm. Unfortunately, many men and horses froze to death under the terrible conditions of that January night.[69]

Nonetheless, Jackson's men endured and the next day pressed on toward Romney. The men who died or became ill due to the freezing weather were taken to the rear, and on January 4, Jackson's men drove the Federal forces out of Bath (now Berkeley Springs). The Confederate force destroyed several train stations and supply depots along the route of the Baltimore and Ohio Railroad, but the stream of unfit soldiers moving to the rear only increased as Jackson got closer to his objective. Many men had severe frostbite and pneumonia and homes along the corridor of

---

[69] Richard A. Sauers, *The Devastating Hand of War: Romney, West Virginia During The Civil War* (Glen Ferris, W.Va.: Gauley Mount Press, 2000), 24.

Jackson's route were packed with sick and frostbitten Confederate soldiers.[70].

Lieutenant "Sandie" Pendleton, of Jackson's staff, suggested that many of the men merely wanted to avoid duty in the frigid conditions, but by January 17, there were approximately 1,700 Confederate soldiers hospitalized in Winchester.[71] According to a soldier in the Stonewall Brigade, as many as ten men died daily of pneumonia in Winchester.[72] Making matters worse, the town was simultaneously contending with an epidemic of scarlet fever.[73]

As Jackson marched toward Romney from Bath, he learned that a brigade of Virginia militia commanded by Brigadier General Gilbert Meem was on its way to Moorefield, about twenty miles south of Romney. Since Meem's militia was in a position to occupy Romney sooner than Jackson, he sent orders for Meem to move into the small town.[74] On January 14, Meem's militia entered Romney and the following day Jackson's troops reached the village.[75]

---

[70] W.G. Bean, *Stonewall's Man: Sandie Pendleton*, (Chapel Hill: The University of North Carolina Press, 1959), 54.

[71] Bean, 54; Delauter, 17.

[72] Robertson, *The Stonewall Brigade*, 65.

[73] Robertson, *The Stonewall Brigade,* 17.

[74] Sauers, 28.

[75] Ibid. According to Sauers the army under Jackson's command did not reach Romney until the 15th of January, some books point to Meems men occupying the town and state that that is when Jackson occupied Romney. Meem was not officially part of Jackson's command; therefore a distinction needs to be made.

Having achieved his objective, Jackson decided not to rest on his good fortune. He thought it prudent to disable several bridges in the area, but the men in his command had enough marching in the cold. The weary soldiers wanted only two things: rest and warmth.[76] Jackson reconsidered and decided not to press the issue any further. His men had accomplished their goal in the face of the greatest adversary of all, Mother Nature.

Jackson placed Loring's troops into defensive positions around Romney and ordered them into winter quarters. On January 23, Jackson and the Stonewall Brigade began their return march to Winchester. He based his decision to take only the Stonewall Brigade back to Winchester on his belief that Loring's men were too broken down and demoralized to reach Winchester.[77]

Loring was upset by the treatment of his command during the campaign and dissension spread rapidly through the ranks. Loring's subordinates took it upon themselves to seek justice in Richmond and their complaints were soon on the desks of Jefferson Davis, Vice President Alexander Stephens, and Secretary of War Judah Benjamin. As a result of these complaints, Benjamin sent a telegram to Jackson on January 31, 1862, ordering Jackson to return Loring to Winchester. Jackson, always obedient to orders, ordered Loring back to Winchester. Once abandoned by Loring, Romney was quickly reoccupied by Federal soldiers.[78]

---

[76] Ibid, 29.

[77] Robertson, *Stonewall Jackson: The Man, The Soldier, The Legend*, 312.

[78] Ibid., 322.

Angered by Benjamin's interference in his command, Jackson submitted his resignation from the Confederate Army.[79]

When the citizens of Winchester learned of Jackson's resignation they denounced Loring and his men for making erroneous accusations against their beloved general. Prominent citizens petitioned Richmond not to remove Jackson from command because they believed that this command change held disaster for the Shenandoah Valley.[80]

News of Jackson's resignation, however, pleased certain Winchester Unionists. Julia Chase wrote: "Gen. Jackson, who has command of the Troops [sic] here, has resigned."[81] Finally in early February, Jackson withdrew his resignation and was once again in full command. Throughout the episode Colonel Alexander Boteler of Jackson's staff and Virginia's Governor Letcher worked hard to convince Confederate officials in Richmond not to accept Jackson's resignation.[82] Jackson appeared to be the only calm participant in the controversy.[83]

---

[79] Ibid., 317.

[80] Henry Kyd Douglas, *I Rode With Stonewall*, (Marietta, Ga.: Mockingbird Books, 1995), 35.

[81] Chase Diary, entry for February 1, 1862.

[82] Robertson, *Stonewall Jackson: The Man, The Soldier, The Legend*, 321. This page describes the tenacity with which Boteler and Letcher fought to retain Jackson. Colonel Boteler served on Jackson's staff and was also a Confederate Congressman from near Shepherdstown, Virginia (later West Virginia). In 1859 he was elected to the United States House of Representatives but after Virginia's secession resigned. He served in the Virginia General Assembly during the war and also was a member of the Confederate Congress. A more thorough description of Boteler can be found in Robertson's biography of Jackson on pages 289-90.

After the resignation issue was resolved it was evident that Jackson and Loring could not cooperate. Loring served in the Mexican War as a major in the regular army, was a decorated hero, and seemed to have real difficulty in subordinating himself to commanders who had served in Mexico as junior officers. Jackson was not the only Confederate officer who experienced problems with Loring; General Robert E. Lee had problems managing the former hero during the failed Northwestern Virginia campaign during the first year of the war.[84] Loring was reassigned to southwestern Virginia by Secretary of War Benjamin and his three brigades were reorganized.[85] Jackson added five of Loring's infantry regiments to his force defending the Lower Shenandoah Valley, increasing his aggregate effective force to approximately 4,600.[86]

On February 25, Major General Nathaniel P. Banks began concentrating his forces at Harpers Ferry; this deployment posed a severe threat to Jackson in nearby Winchester. One week later, Banks had massed 36,000 men who were strategically positioned at Hapers Ferry, as well as Martinsburg, and at Charles Town, and

---

[83] Robertson, *Stonewall Jackson: The Man, The Soldier, The Legend*, 318. Reverend Graham was the one to whom the comment is attributed.

[84] For more information on the problems that General Lee faced with General Loring see, Freeman, *R.E. Lee*, 1:550-52.

[85] Bean, 55; Sauers, 24. When Loring came to reinforce Jackson at Winchester in December 1861, he brought three brigades from his Army of the Northwest.

[86] Robertson, *Stonewall Jackson: The Man, The Soldier, The Legend*, 321. The units that Jackson gained from Loring's command were the 21st, 42nd, 48th Regiments of Virginia infantry, the 1st Battalion of Virginia infantry, and the Fredericksburg and Danville Artillery batteries.

were poised to strike at Winchester. It was clear to Jackson that Winchester could not be defended against a force of that magnitude.

Many of Winchester's residents, frightened at the prospect of being placed under Union control, intended to leave before the Yankees arrived. Jubilant at the prospect of a Union occupation, Union sympathizer Julia Chase wrote:

> Quite a number of people are leaving town, frightened almost to death of the Yankees, that they will come and catch them. Dr. McGuire has sent his family off and says he intends burning his house.[87]

Tears were shed as friends parted for who knew how long? Perhaps no departure, however, was filled with more emotion than Jackson's separation from his wife, Mary Anna.

A Union brigade under the command of Brigadier General Alpheus Williams was positioned north of Winchester at Bunker Hill on March 6. The following day Williams moved his brigade forward to Stephenson's Depot, slightly north of Winchester. On the same day, a body of Union troops skirmished with Turner Ashby's cavalry at Stephenson's and after an inconclusive fight the Federal soldiers rejoined Banks' main force.

Jackson stubbornly offered battle to General Banks north of town, but the cautious Banks declined to attack without General

---

[87] Chase Diary, Entry for March 3, 1862.

James Shields' division at his disposal.[88] Banks finally positioned his entire force north of Winchester on March 11. He intended to attack Jackson on that day, but General Williams first went forward under a flag of truce to warn the townspeople that if they wanted to be safe they should leave Winchester.[89] With battle impending and occupation imminent the citizens made final attempts to secure their most valuable possessions. On that day, a staunch Confederate, Mrs. Hugh Lee, unequaled in her support for the Confederate cause, wrote: "From twelve till after one, we were very busy, putting in place of safety, silver, papers, sword, flags… clothes, war letters…"[90]

Also that day Jackson issued orders for his army to withdraw to the south. In a council of war with his commanders Jackson speculated his troops marching south might be recalled to deliver battle during the night. The men, however, had marched too far and Jackson abandoned the idea.

As Jackson moved south, General Banks prepared to capture the town. At 9 a.m. on March 12, Banks entered town ready to fight, but to his amazement found that Jackson's force had withdrawn.[91] Only elements of Turner Ashby's cavalry remained

---

[88] Robertson, *The Stonewall Brigade*, 69.

[89] Delauter, 19.

[90] Mrs. Hugh Lee, Diary March 11, 1862 – November 17, 1865. 1182 WFCHS-Mrs. Hugh Lee Collection, Box 1, Handley Archives, entry is for March 11, 1862.

[91] Brooke, journal entry for March 12, 1862.

after Jackson's main force pulled out of Winchester and Ashby's men left an hour before Banks' arrival.[92]

The morning Banks entered Winchester several Confederate cavalryman watched for the Stars and Stripes to be unfurled – "they dashed down towards them as far as the Court House..." wrote Kate Sperry.[93] These brave and foolish men were greeted by a Union soldier, a former resident of the town named Jenkins, he "waved his hands to our men and begged them for God's sake to leave for the Yankees had sent a detachment down the back street to flank them – it is needless to say they left."[94]

Although he fought no battle to secure the town, Banks entered triumphantly, "in a most martial manner... riding in a carriage drawn by four white mules."[95]   The jubilant Unionist, Julia Chase, was overjoyed at the sight of Union soldiers and wrote: "Glorious news, The Union Army took possession of Winchester today and the glorious old flag is waving over town."[96]

John Peyton Clark, a member of the town's Confederate majority, recorded the events of March 12:

> ...Federal troops entered Winchester. Their first
> appearance within the limits of the town was made
> by a small body of cavalry down Market Street
> followed almost immediately by a squad of infantry
> in blue uniforms numbering perhaps forty men...

---

[92] Bean, 334.
[93] Sperry, diary entry for March 12, 1862.
[94] Ibid.
[95] Brooke, journal entry for March 12, 1862.
[96] Chase, diary entry for March 12, 1862.

About ten o'clock the panorama commenced, melancholy and distressing enough to all good citizens. Regiment after regiment filed by, each preceded by a band of music discoursing "Hail Columbia, Happy Land" The town during the entrance presented a sad and sullen appearance. Many of the houses of the citizens were entirely closed, few, perhaps none of the respectable portion of the town were conspicuous on the street, no gratification was expressed but decidedly the contrary sentiment evinced unmistakably to them, and although they were greeted in some individual cases by citizens and negro men and women who were congregated on the corners of the streets for the purpose, yet the character of those extending the greeting was such as to be immediately recognized and evidently afforded them no care for self–congratulation.[97]

Mrs. Lee could only write: "All is over and we are prisoners in our own houses…"[98]

The Union Army destroyed property during their first occupation of Winchester in a way that shocked observers. Although much worse was to come later in the war, the destruction of 1862 was without precedent for Winchester's citizens.[99] "This is barbarous beyond description…", wrote Mr. Clark.[100] On the

---

[97] John Peyton Clark, Journal, March 12, 1862 – September 15, 1862. 424 WFCHS, Louisa Crawford Collection, Box 1, Handley Archives, diary entry for March 12, 1862.

[98] Lee, diary entry for March 12, 1862.

[99] Property was not destroyed on a grand scale as it would be during 1863 and 1864, however, this was the first Union occupation that the townspeople endured and any destruction of private property was shocking. Confiscating livestock and damaging farms was a common practice among Banks' troops.

[100] Clark, diary entry for March 14, 1862.

first day of Banks' occupation, two Union soldiers ascended Mr. Clark's porch steps and knocked on his door. Infuriated, he went to the door. He wrote:

> … I immediately went out and confronted the two at the parlor door. I asked them what they wanted here. They said they had come to see if this house was occupied. I replied that it was and no accommodations could be had. They said they meant no offense and retired…[101]

Unfortunately for the townspeople, not all of the Union soldiers were as polite as this pair.

While the citizens of the town endured what they viewed as treachery, their hearts and prayers remained with Jackson and his army. Mrs. Lee noted: "I remembered how thankful I was that Jackson had not risked a battle, and that our precious little army was safe."[102]

---

[101] Clark., diary entry for March 14, 1862 reads: "Visitors now frequent at the front door for accomodations [sic] and at the kitchen door for bread and meat.."
[102] Lee, diary entry for March 12, 1862.

Major General Nathaniel P. Banks, the first Union commander at Winchester. Banks served as governor of Massachusetts from 1858-1861. When the war broke out he was given the rank of Major General by President Abraham Lincoln. Like so many Union generals, Banks received his military rank only through his ties with the Republican Party. After being defeated by Stonewall Jackson in the Shenandoah Valley, Banks confronted Jackson at the Battle of Cedar Mountain, August 9, 1862. Banks was lambasted for making poor tactical decisions during the battle. After Cedar Mountain he commanded the Department of the Gulf. He left the army after a failed attempt to occupy northwestern Louisiana in 1864. After the Civil War he served six terms in the United States House of Representatives. He died in 1894 in Waltham, Massachusetts. (Handley Regional Library)

One of the most common burdens on the townspeople was the Federal search of homes for Confederate symbols or supplies for Rebel soldiers. An incident occurred at the Clark home on March 14, in which a Union soldier searched for a fictitious secessionist flag "which he understood was in the house…

threatening to blow out the d[amne]d brains of Sarah if she told him a lie and did not get it for him."[103]

The frightened citizens rarely left the somewhat secure confines of their homes. It was rare to see more than a handful of people in the streets at any one time because many inhabitants only left their abodes out of pure necessity.[104]

Union officers, however, demanded discipline in the ranks and worked to control the rowdy behavior of enlisted men. Officers attempted, often unsuccessfully, to instill a sense of security and safety in the townspeople.[105] Mr. Clark, for example, viewed Federal soldiers as the lowest form of human life: "The meanness of these wretches is inconceivable and scarcely comprehensible to one who has not associated all his life with highway robbers and pick pockets."[106]

Union soldiers routinely stole from various stores. Nighttime brought out the worst in these soldiers. Soldiers stayed up into the late hours of the night and made such commotion as to awaken the dead. "… We have been very much annoyed tonight by some of these ruffians sitting upon the front porch steps and

---

[103] Clark, diary entry for March 14, 1862.

[104] Ibid., diary entry for March 20, 1862. The entry reads "… few citizens, except in cases of necessity, are now seen on the street."

[105] Minrose C. Gwin, ed., *A Woman's Civil War: A Diary, with Reminiscences of War, from March 1862* (Madison: University of Wisconsin Press, 1992), 27. In this passage Cornelia McDonald describes a confrontation that she had with a Union officer who ensured her that no harm was to come to her.

[106] Clark, diary entry for March 20, 1862.

singing songs and exhibiting a profanity which was revolting," wrote Mr. Clark. [107]

Six days after Banks' arrival, Brigadier General James Shields' division marched south, up the Valley on an expedition. Shields marched his men only as far as Strasburg when he decided to return to Winchester, and his regiments reached that place on March 20. Banks' superiors seemed to think that he did not need three divisions to contend with Jackson. Two of his divisions were released to reinforce General George B. McClellan in eastern Virginia, while Shields' division remained to protect Winchester. Banks believed that Jackson's small force was no threat to Winchester, thereby grossly underestimating the impact this decision would have on the ensuing Valley campaign

Colonel Turner Ashby's cavalry kept a keen eye on Banks' movement and immediately sent word to Jackson of the withdrawal of Banks' divisions. With the departure of Union forces from Strasburg and the news of the withdrawal of two divisions from Winchester's defenses, the moment Jackson had waited for arrived. Jackson moved his men north immediately and by the evening of March 22, arrived near Strasburg. [108]

Ashby's cavalry proceeded north on the morning of March 22, with a force of 290 men and Captain R. Preston Chew's

---

[107] Ibid., diary entry for March 21, 1862.
[108] Delauter, 22.

Artillery.[109]   As this force moved toward the town, people along their route confirmed Ashby's estimate that he faced only a force of four regiments.[110]   Turner Ashby's informants were gravely mistaken as General Shields' entire division rested comfortably just north of Winchester.

A body of Union cavalrymen under the command of Major Angelo Paldi picketed the Valley Pike two miles south of Winchester and as Union pickets patrolled and watered their horses at Abraham's Creek, they heard the approach of Ashby's cavalry.[111]   Surprised, the pickets fell back closer to town, and were quickly reinforced.   Later in the afternoon, a successful Union counterattack forced Ashby's horsemen to withdraw.[112]

Near the end of the engagement General Shields, who was with Battery H, 1st Ohio Light Artillery, was wounded in the arm by a shell fragment.[113]   Command of the division was transferred to Colonel Nathan Kimball, Shields' second-in-command.   That evening the hopes of Confederates in Winchester grew as Jackson's force was near and poised to retake the town.

During the early morning hours of Sunday, March 23, Jackson formed his men and marched to Kernstown, located slightly south of Abraham's Creek and several miles south of

---

[109] Gary L Ecelbarger, *"We are in for it!": The First Battle of Kernstown,* (Shippensburg, Pa.: White Mane Publishing, 1997), 68.
[110] Delauter, 22; Ecelbarger, 68.
[111] Ecelbarger, 68.
[112] Ibid., 70.
[113] Ibid., 71.

Winchester along the Valley Pike. Jackson reached there at approximately 1 p.m. and met Turner Ashby who insisted that the reports he sent to Jackson on March 20, were genuine: there was only a token force defending Winchester.[114]

Jackson saw both opportunity and necessity at Kernstown. Based on Ashby's intelligence, Jackson had an opportunity to strike a numerically inferior force and carry out his strategic role in the Shenandoah Valley – holding Yankee forces there. Jackson knew that as long as he was in the Shenandoah Valley only limited numbers of Union reinforcements could be sent to Union Major General George B. McClellan, who had been massing an army of 105,000 men on the Virginia peninsula since March in preparation to strike Richmond. If the Union forces had already withdrawn – as Turner Ashby reported – Jackson needed to order an attack.

The Union force at Kernstown was twice the size Jackson had expected, however, and as the battle raged, the townspeople of Winchester listened to the roar of cannon and musketry as they prayed for the liberation of their town. Minute by minute the fire south of town intensified. It slackened in the evening and soon ceased, signaling the withdrawal of Jackson's army. Jackson had been defeated and Winchester remained in Union hands. Although defeated tactically at Kernstown Jackson lost no confidence in himself or his army.

---

[114] Delauter, 23. This refers specifically to the time that Jackson arrived at Kernstown.

Through the night of March 23 and the following day, Winchester again became a hospital for battlefield casualties. The day following the battle Mr. Clark reported the horrific scene:

> The ambulances have been running all the day to the battle – field bringing in the wounded. The Court House, York House, Union Hotel, Rouss' Store and house, and other houses are filled, presenting every variety of wound, some of them shocking and distressing to the last degree.[115]

According to Kate Sperry, 200 Confederate prisoners were brought into Winchester the day after the battle along with approximately twenty-five wounded Confederate soldiers.[116] While the Confederate prisoners waited for transport to a Federal prison camp, local citizens sought access to the prisoners. Although at first denied, Union officers later granted permission.[117]

During the afternoon of March 24, the Confederate prisoners were marched to the train depot and their passage became a kind of parade. Winchester's citizens lined the streets and handed out biscuits and other food to the weary soldiers, some of which were town residents. Gripped by the scene of familiar faces passing as prisoners of war, Mr. Clark penned:

---

[115] Clark, diary entry for March 24, 1862.
[116] Sperry, diary entry for March 24, 1862, it reads as follows: "The whole town is full of dead and wounded Yanks – they took 200 of our men prisoners and have about 25 wounded of ours besides."
[117] Delauter, 23.

> ... Among these were some of our dear friends.
> The prisoners were greeted by the ladies of the town
> with much feeling and boldness from their front
> doors and porches as they passed up Market Street
> to the depot for transportation north... The ladies
> held out baskets of biscuits and perhaps other things
> which they took as they moved along...[118]

While the people of Winchester were not strangers to war's carnage, this time they saw and experienced the immediate aftermath of a large battle. The sights that confronted those tending to the wounded men were sickening. Although most of the women of Winchester despised anyone in a Federal uniform, their collective sense of charity and human decency was quite apparent. Many women pitied the men in blue who were dying without any loved ones to hold their hands during their final moments. The merciful women of Winchester did what was possible to ease their pain. The sight of casualties on the steps of the courthouse was heart-breaking; dead Union soldiers lay there with the capes of their overcoats covering their faces.[119] Some had small pieces of paper attached to their uniform to identify them while others lay nameless.

The First Battle of Kernstown was seen as a great victory for the Union and the victory prompted a visit by two members of President Abraham Lincoln's cabinet, Secretary of State William Seward and Secretary of War Edwin Stanton. Both officials

---

[118] Clark, diary entry for March 24, 1862.

[119] Gwin, ed., 37. Cornelia McDonald describes her experiences at the Court House in the aftermath of the First Battle of Kernstown.

arrived in Winchester during the night of March 28, and on the following day they toured the Kernstown battlefield. Disgusted at the presence of these men, Kate Sperry wrote: "Old Seward and Stanton – Sec. Of State and Sec. of War came this evening to visit us and the battlefield – the old 'rips' – to think our soil should ever be desecrated by the tread of such black hearted villains."[120]

A Union victory and the sight of two top government officials brought despair to the secessionists of Winchester, but for the handful of Union supporters they brought increased hope. "Town quiet, no news, everything depressed and sad except the countenance of a half dozen Unionists who seem to be satisfied and even rejoice over their own slavery..." wrote Mr. Clark.[121]

General Banks did not begin pursuing Jackson's forces until several weeks later. As an occupying force, he left the 110th Regiment Pennsylvania Volunteer Infantry and the First Regiment Potomac Home Brigade under the command of Colonel William D. Lewis.[122] Military disorder spread throughout the garrison force in Winchester as men neglected guard duties and caused a great number of disturbances.

Nevertheless, the women of Winchester persisted with daily duties and acts of mercy. There were still many injured soldiers recuperating in hospitals in the town. Mrs. Lee noted: "This is surely the day of woman's power; the men are afraid to

---

[120] Sperry, diary entry for March 28, 1862.
[121] Clark, diary entry for March 31, 1862.
[122] Delauter, 24-25. According to the author the administrative skills of Colonel Lewis were quite ineffective.

do, or say, anything, & leave all to us".[123]   The women's work eased after the arrival of Dorthea Dix and her nursing assistants.

Shortly after Fort Sumter, Dix volunteered her nursing services to the federal government and, in June 1861, she was given authority by Secretary of War Simon Cameron to manage all nurses in the service of the army. Dix received no pay for her services. The arrival of her nursing corps alleviated the heavy burden on the women of Winchester. Mrs. Lee, elated at the arrival of this "good Samaritan" wrote: "Miss Dix has come & brought a corps of nurses, & to my inexpressible relief, I shall not have to go to the Hospital again, unless something unforseen [sic] occurs."[124]

Conditions improved somewhat in Winchester after General Shields relieved Colonel Lewis as post commander on April 18, with Lieutenant Colonel Thomas McDowell of the 84th Regiment Pennsylvania Volunteer Infantry. McDowell was more lenient toward the citizens and earned a reputation for fairness in deciding issues brought to his attention. However, on May 9, another post commander, Colonel George Beal of the 10th Regiment Maine Infantry, took command of the town's garrison and he proved much harsher than his predecessor. [125]

On May 16, the Winchester Medical College paid a heavy price for purloining the corpse of Watson Brown – it was burned to

---

[123] Lee, diary entry for April 1, 1862.
[124] Ibid.
[125] Delauter, 26. The information contained throughout the paragraph is derived from this page.

the ground. Brown, a son of John Brown, was killed in the 1859 raid on Harpers Ferry and the corpse was taken from Harpers Ferry by students of the Winchester Medical College for study. Mr. Clark, outraged at the destruction of the Medical College wrote:

> Last night the Yankees set fire to the building of the medical college. The incendiary act is supposed to have originated in revenge for the fact that the body of old John Brown's son who was killed at Harpers Ferry was carried there as a subject for dissection, and whose skeleton was there at the time of the fire…there is reason to believe that this act was done by order, or at least with the concurrence of the commandant of the Post, Col. Beale [sic] of the 10th Maine Reg… and although three of the fire engines of the town were taken to the spot, they remained inactive there during the whole time of the burning…[126]

In early May news came that Jackson was again on the offensive. On May 8, he defeated Federal forces at the Battle of McDowell. After the defeat, General Banks withdrew his forces north to Strasburg. There, Banks fortified his position and deployed a detachment to Front Royal to protect the Manassas Gap Railroad. The following days brought a heightened sense of optimism to the Confederates of Winchester as they learned of the possibility that Jackson would make another effort to reclaim Winchester.

---

[126] Clark, diary entry for May 17, 1862.

Winchester's citizens were elated with Jackson's victory at McDowell. While many townspeople prepared and hoped for his arrival in Winchester, Jackson was marching north with a large force. On May 21, Jackson and General Richard S. Ewell combined their forces near Luray and two days later overwhelmed the Union garrison at Front Royal, capturing that force at Cedarville.[127] Jackson was now only ten miles from Banks and fifteen miles from Winchester.[128] The aggressive Confederate commander now held the advantage; his force outnumbered Banks' by a margin of about two to one.[129]

Later that afternoon Charles Greenleaf, a Union cavalryman, greeted Banks at Strasburg with news of events that transpired earlier in the day. Following Greenleaf's report, General Banks decided it best to pull back from Strasburg to Winchester. Banks' army marched into Winchester during the evening of May 24, and Mrs. Lee, longing for an end to Banks' presence, wrote in her diary:

---

[127] Robert G. Tanner, *Stonewall in the Valley: Thomas J. 'Stonewall' Jackson's Shenandoah Valley Campaign, Spring 1862* (Garden City: Doubleday & Company, Inc., 1976), 203. In reference to the date Jackson and Ewell combined forces.

[128] William Allen, *History of the Campaign of Gen. T.J. (Stonewall) Jackson in the Shenandoah Valley of Virginia From November 4, 1861 – June 17, 1862* (Dayton, Oh.: Morningside, 1991), 98.

[129] James M. McPherson, *Battle Cry of Freedom* (New York: Ballantine Books, 1998), 456.

> During the whole day, Bank's [sic] army has been coming in & he & his staff arrived this evening. They are either preparing for an immediate evacuation, or for a fight; God grant it maybe the former.[130]

The optimism of Winchester's citizens increased as they heard the news of Jackson's victory at Front Royal the previous day. The townspeople knew that Jackson's pursuit of Banks' battered force might liberate the town.

As Banks fell back to Winchester, four companies of cavalry arrived from Harpers Ferry to bolster his ranks.[131] As Jackson moved closer to Winchester on the night of May 24, General Banks calmly waited for his hot bath to be readied at the Taylor Hotel.[132]

Banks' defensive positions on high ground stretched for nearly two and a half miles along the north side of Abraham's Creek, with his left flank anchored near the Front Royal Road and the right of his line stretching west of the Valley Pike.[133] The artillery posted on Camp Hill and Bowers Hill compensated for Banks' numerical weakness. The Union troops stood to arms through the night of May 24, and gazed into the distance at the flickering fires of their gathering Confedarate foes.[134]

---

[130] Lee, diary entry for May 24, 1862.

[131] Brandon H. Beck & Charles S. Grunder, *The First Battle of Winchester* (Lynchburg, Va.: H.E. Howard, 1992), 47.

[132] Ibid.

[133] Beck and Grunder, *The First Battle of Winchester*, 48.

[134] Ibid.

At daybreak, the Confederates launched their attack against the Union defensive line. Jackson advanced along the Valley Pike while Ewell attacked from the Front Royal Road toward Union defenses on Camp Hill. At first light, picket firing opened the engagement and was soon followed by artillery fire.[135] As the Union artillery roared, the gray-clad infantry moved to attack Banks on two fronts.

On the right, Brigadier General Isaac Trimble's brigade of Ewell's division advanced through a heavy morning fog that was soon darkened by black powder smoke. Trimble's brigade was surprised by a Union regiment of Colonel Dudley Donnely's brigade and the 21st North Carolina and the 21st Georgia regiments bore the brunt of its destructive fire.[136] The two Confederate regiments advanced under a galling fire delivered by the 28th New York and 46th Pennsylvania Infantry. The pair of regiments -- Trimble called them "my two 21's" -- advanced oblivious to the fact that in their immediate front lay the 5th Connecticut Infantry. As the distance closed, the Connecticut regiment rose and delivered a devastating volley that hurled Trimble's regiments backward. The aggressive Connecticut soldiers surged forward after firing and forced the "two 21's" further back. In order for Trimble to attack again he needed the other two regiments of his

---

[135] U.S. War Department (comp.), *War of the Rebellion: A Compilation of the Official Records of the Union and Confederate Armies* Ser. I, Vol. XII, Pt. 1, (Washington: U.S. Government Printing Office, 1880 – 1901), 528. Cited hereafter as *O.R.*, report of the battle by General N.P. Banks.
[136] Beck and Grunder, *The First Battle of Winchester*, 51.

brigade, the 15th Alabama and the 16th Mississippi, neither of which was then in position to attack.[137] Jackson soon concluded that the Union position on Camp Hill could not be taken. If the Confederates were to win the battle and liberate Winchester, Jackson had to strike the western end of the Union line solidly situated on top of Bowers Hill.

While Jackson had a numerical advantage in artillery, the Federals held the advantage of terrain and had rifled guns on Bowers Hill. Two sections of the 1st New York Artillery, a section of Hampton's Maryland Battery, and Best's Battery held the hill.[138] Jackson knew the key to the battle was Bowers Hill and he turned to his former command, the Stonewall Brigade, now commanded by General Charles S. Winder, and ordered them to take the ridge.[139]

The Stonewall Brigade stepped off to attack in nearly perfect alignment. The assault went smoothly for Winder until his men began to climb the slopes. As the brigade ascended the hill, it was struck by a hail of lead and iron from Union artillery and infantry located on the crest of the ridge and was pinned down.

---

[137] Beck and Grunder, *The First Battle of Winchester*, 52.
[138] Ibid., 52-3. The 1st New York employed the use of 6 pound Parrot Rifles.
[139] Editors of Time Life Books, *Voices of the Civil War: Shenandoah 1862* (Alexandria: Time Life Books, 1997), 93. Robertson, *The Stonewall Brigade*, 94. The Brigade advanced in the following order, 5th Virginia deployed as skirmishers, 27th Virginia deployed to the left, the 2nd Virginia deployed to the right of the 27th Virginia, the 4th Virginia deployed to the right of the 2nd Virginia and the 33rd Virginia was held in reserve.

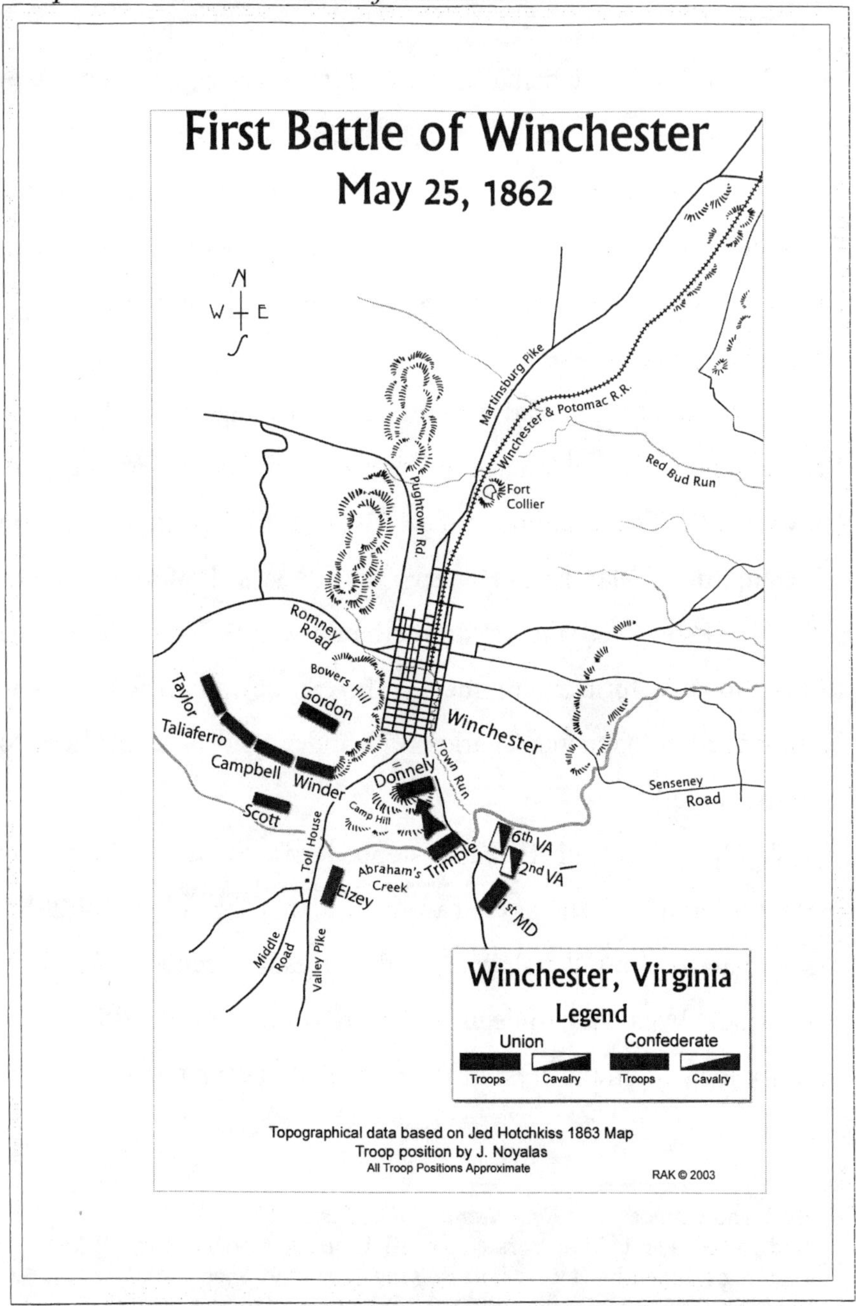

Early on the morning of May 25, 1862, Confederate forces under command of Stonewall Jackson moved to attack General Nathaniel P. Banks at Winchester. While Jackson moved to Winchester on the Valley Pike, Confederate forces under command of General Richard S. Ewell marched on the Front Royal Road. Banks' men retreated through the streets of Winchester and were pursued by Jackson's men as far as Stephenson's Depot, located several miles north of town.

With the Stonewall Brigade in trouble, Jackson ordered a heavy flank attack, a tactic soon to become his trademark. To turn Banks' right flank, Jackson chose Brigadier General Richard Taylor's Louisiana Brigade. Taylor marched his men westward along Abraham's Creek to a point where it emerged in a hollow depression where it was joined by two regiments of Brigadier General William Taliaferro's brigade.[140] Taylor's force readied itself for an assault, but was exposed to Union artillery fire. General Taylor saw some men dodging the shells and yelled profanities at them for their behavior.[141] General Jackson, who was nearby, heard the cursing, glared at Taylor with reproach, and told him he was a wicked fellow before riding away.[142]

Taylor's brigade prepared to advance and with the support of the Rockbridge Artillery the Southerners surged forward in a well-disciplined assault. The Confederate brigade stepped off at approximately 7:30 a.m. and swiftly gathered momentum. Under a heavy fire, the Louisiana Brigade rushed forward as Union cavalry stormed down the slopes on Taylor's left in a counterattack, but were repulsed by Lieutenant Colonel Francis T. Nicholls' 8th Louisiana Infantry.[143] The boys from Louisiana performed admirably in this battle.

---

[140] Beck & Grunder, _The First Battle of Winchester_, 55.
[141] T. Michael Parrish, *Richard Taylor: Soldier Prince of Dixie* (Chapel Hill: University of North Carolina Press, 1992), 183.
[142] *Voices of Valor: Shenandoah 1862*, 93.
[143] Parrish, 185-86.

As the Rebels advanced toward the Union line, many Federal soldiers took to their heels and fled toward safety even before the Confederates reached the crest of the hill.[144]

While the rout of Union forces developed on Jackson's left, General Ewell, on the right also managed to outflank Banks. Defeated Union soldiers fled through the streets of Winchester as Jackson pressed forward in pursuit. Two regiments, the 5th and the 27th Virginia Infantry, had the distinction of being the first Confederates to enter Winchester. "In the course of half or three quarters of an hour from the time the Confederates entered the town on the south side it was cleared of Federal troops", remembered Mr. Clark.[145] Many of Winchester's citizens, overjoyed at the return of Jackson, and his army and the defeat of the Federals, rushed into the streets to greet them. The townspeople urged Jackson's men forward and in a number of instances soldiers had to hold their fire to avoid injuring innocent bystanders. Some civilians remained indoors and took some well-aimed shots at the fleeing Union soldiers.[146]

Unable to escape, many Federals fell captive. The Confederates abandoned their pursuit after reaching Stephenson's Depot. With his infantry and artillery exhausted and lacking sufficient cavalry to pursue, Jackson lost the opportunity to annihilate Banks. Jackson's command set up camp five miles

---

[144] Robertson, *The Stonewall Brigade*, 96.
[145] Clark, journal entry for May 26, 1862.
[146] Delauter., 30.

north of town while Banks marched his remaining troops twenty-two miles north to Martinsburg where he arrived at 2:40 p.m. on May 25.[147]

General Banks, although able to save the remnants of his army, left behind a large amount of supplies and 3,000 prisoners, including forty-two officers.[148] In the captured military stores were 500,000 rounds of ammunition, over 100 cattle, and 14,600 pounds of bacon.[149] While Jackson was frustrated by the necessity of halting his columns, the town's citizens now enjoyed the presence of many of their loved ones who were serving in his army. A much relieved Mrs. Lee wrote two days later: "the battle has been fought; the victory won; we are free; our precious soldiers are here, in Winchester, with us all the time, morning & night…"[150]

There were some families in mourning, however. Most notable was the Barton family that had six sons fighting for the Confederacy. Early in the engagement, Charles Marshall Barton, a lieutenant in Cutshaw's Artillery, fell mortally wounded near Hollingsworth's Mill.[151] Charles' body was brought to his home and was placed in the room in which he was born.[152]

---

[147] Ibid., 30; Beck and Grunder, *The First Battle of Winchester,* 60; *O.R.,* Ser. I, Vol. XII, Part 1, 528. Report of General N.P. Banks at Martinsburg.
[148] Sperry, diary entry for May 31, 1862.
[149] Robertson, *Stonewall Jackson, The Man, The Soldier, The Legend,* 411.
[150] Lee, diary entry for May 27, 1862.
[151] Margaretta Barton Colt, *Defend the Valley: A Shenandoah Family in the Civil War* (Oxford: Oxford University Press, 1994), 149-50. This includes a number

Although the majority of townspeople were elated at the Confederate's return, some of the town's Union supporters fled. Among those who left with Banks' force was Charles Chase, who had just been appointed the new town postmaster by President Lincoln. He had held his office for one day.[153]

On May 27, Turner Ashby was promoted to brigadier general. Jackson's aide, Sandie Pendleton, presented the flamboyant cavalier his new rank in a brief ceremony in the Taylor Hotel. General Ashby held this rank for a brief time before being killed near Harrisonburg on June 6, while fighting a rearguard action. Although Jackson had differences with Ashby – especially over what he saw as the lack of discipline in Ashby's troops -- he grieved at his death.[154] Ashby's body was moved to Winchester from Charlottesville on October 25, 1866, and interred in the Stonewall Cemetery near his brother Richard (also brought to Winchester on October 25, 1866) who also had been killed in the war.

After a stay of several days, Jackson was ordered by the War Department to move against Harpers Ferry and give the impression that his army might march into Maryland or attack the Union capital.[155] On May 28, his gray-clad soldiers marched out

---

of the letters and memoirs of members of the Barton family who served the Confederacy; Beck and Grunder, *The First Battle Of Winchester*, 62.

[152] Beck and Grunder, *The First Battle of Winchester*, 62.

[153] Sperry, diary entry for May 28, 1863.

[154] Millard K. Bushong, *General Turner Ashby and Stonewall's Valley Campaign* (Waynesboro, Va.: The McClung Corporation, 1992), 183.

[155] Robertson, *Stonewall Jackson: The Man, The Soldier, The Legend*, 413.

of town in the direction of Harpers Ferry. Only the 21st Virginia remained to defend Winchester. Jackson was now going to prey on the worst fears of Northern politicians by placing their capital in danger.

Jackson's victory at Winchester greatly benefited General Joseph E. Johnston's Confederate forces defending Richmond because it altered the Union Army's strategic situation. In order to protect the capital a portion of Major General Irvin McDowell's command was recalled from Fredericksburg to the defense of the capital.[156] Jackson's victory at Winchester effectively removed any possibility of McDowell moving on Richmond and aiding McClellan's push to Richmond via the Virginia peninsula.[157]

In Winchester, Mrs. Lee feared that the large number of Union prisoners held in the front of the courthouse yard might cause a disturbance; the prisoners were more numerous than their guards.[158] The Confederate movement toward Harpers Ferry was only hours old when Jackson received information that fresh Union forces were approaching Strasburg. Two Union armies, General Shields' from the east and General John C. Fremont's from the

---

[156] On the night of May 25, Secretary of War Edwin Stanton telegraphed Assistant Secretary John Tucker at Fort Monroe: "A part of McDowell's force has been recalled to this city. Our condition is one of considerable danger, as we are stripped to supply the Army of the Potomac..." *O.R.* Ser. I, Vol. XII, Part 3, 241.

[157] Beck and Grunder, *The First Battle of Winchester,* 64-5. For a complete study of how Jackson's victory at Winchester altered the strategic situation for the Union army see; Stephen W. Sears, *To the Gates of Richmond: The Peninsula Campaign* (New York: Ticknor and Fields, 1992), 110-12.

[158] Lee, diary entry for May 28, 1862.

west, were rapidly converging on the lower Shenandoah Valley town and if Jackson did not move quickly he risked being trapped in the lower Shenandoah Valley.[159]

Jackson was loath to give up Winchester, but was left with no alternative. He returned to Winchester and marched his forces out of town on May 31. The Stonewall Brigade was the last Confederate unit to leave Winchester.

As Jackson's troops marched south, Winchester's citizens realized that the town's door was again wide open for the Federals. Jackson did move the Union captives out of Winchester to prison camps, but a saddened Kate Sperry, on that somber day, wrote: "… our town is mostly cleared – all the prisoners were marched off today – they've been bragging so much about going to Richmond – they'll get there in a different way than they anticipated…"[160]

During the next two days Winchester waited for the Federals and the return of the ravages of war. In the early hours of June 3, Union cavalry entered the town as the vanguard of the large Union force that arrived on June 4.[161] Acts of revenge against the citizens of the town by Union soldiers were again committed. Reverend Brooke wrote: "Soldiers killing hogs, lambs – stealing horses in every direction – everybody molested – women struck by soldiers".[162] For the town's inhabitants nothing was

---

[159] Delauter, 34.
[160] Sperry, diary entry for May 31, 1862.
[161] Delauter, 35.
[162] Brooke, journal entry for June 10, 1862.

sacred to the Union soldiers. Businesses and private homes were robbed, and an infuriated Mr. Clark recollected:

> ... The conduct of these men after their entrance was characterized by every species of outrage and violence upon the citizens of the town short of actual murder. Their former behavior was mild and gentle compared with their conduct now.[163]

German-born Major General Franz Sigel was in temporary command of the town and set up his headquarters in the Taylor Hotel. After finding the hotel's furniture not to his taste, Sigel decided to do a little interior decorating, but did not have the budget for it. On June 7, the ill-mannered German went to the home of Mrs. Lloyd Logan, where he picked out furniture from her home and had the pieces taken to the Taylor Hotel to furnish his quarters.[164] With the Union Army back in town, many of the Union sympathizers also returned on the same day.[165]

During the next several months most of the town's citizens endured the Union presence; soldiers became rowdy in the streets and civilians were little more than prisoners in their own homes. Worse still, some individuals had their homes commandeered for military use. Surviving these trying months, however, hardened the town's residents for the ensuing years of conflict.

---

[163] Clark, diary entry for June 9, 1862.
[164] Delauter, 36.
[165] Chase, diary entry for June 7, 1862.

Jackson's Shenandoah Valley Campaign was masterful. He marched his force more than 600 miles in about forty-five days and defeated three different Union armies while preventing reinforcements from reaching Major General George B. McClellan who was then threatening Richmond from the Virginia peninsula. It was this campaign that gave Jackson legendary status in the annals of military history. Jackson's strategic genius lives on today for his classic Valley Campaign is studied at military academies and senior service schools around the world.

Following Jackson's victorious Valley Campaign the battered Federal Army concentrated around Winchester. The townspeople rejoiced over Jackson's victories, but deeply resented the presence of the Union Army, particularly when Union soldiers increased their "punishment" of Winchester's residents. For example, Mrs. Logan was subjected to further hardship. After losing some of her finest pieces of furniture to Sigel, she became a prisoner in her own home. General John P. Hatch occupied her house for use as a headquarters and the "generous" Hatch graciously allowed Mrs. Logan and her family only two rooms in which to reside.[166]

---

[166] Delauter, 36

Numerous similar incidents occurred throughout the town. A frequent outrage involved commandeering private property. In mid-June, Mr. Clark received some Union officers at his home that requested the use of his home as a headquarters. Disgusted over this and previous intrusions, Clark visited General Banks to complain.[167] After returning from his meeting with Banks, Clark recorded the substance of the meeting in his diary.

> I went to see General Banks and stated the case to him. He said no authority had been given to turn anyone out of their homes, but if I had any vacant rooms he would advise me to let them upon application to officers of the army for which they must pay full price.[168]

While Banks glossed over the way in which the commandeering system operated, it is clear through the actions of Sigel and Hatch that Banks' order was treated as a recommendation, not an order by his subordinates.

Commandeering property, theft, and other similar acts culminated in bloodshed on the night of June 11, at the Baker and Brothers' store and warehouse on North Cameron Street.[169] On several earlier occasions, Union soldiers had broken into the store and damaged or looted its contents. The exasperated owner acquired a pass permitting him to post an armed guard at the store.

---

[167] It is difficult to say who retained control of Winchester at this time. Sigel was in command in the opening days of June, however Banks appears to have been in control on the day of Clark's complaint.

[168] Clark, diary entry for June 16, 1862.

[169] Sperry, diary entry for June 12, 1862

During that June night, several Federal soldiers made an attempt to break into the store, but these Union marauders were unaware of the guard hired by the proprietor.[170] The guard, a man named Striker, warned the intruders to halt, but they persisted.[171] Striker then shot and killed one of the trespassers.[172]

To retaliate for the soldier's death Union soldiers set fire to the store and warehouse about 9 a.m. the next morning.[173] "The Yanks very quietly stuffed straw in the house and burnt it to the ground," remembered Kate Sperry in her diary.[174] The blaze threatened convalescing soldiers in the nearby Union Hotel, but fortunately, the wounded and sick were evacuated quickly and the hotel was saved. Only a single casualty resulted from the fire. As the warehouse blazed, a Union soldier ran into the inferno to loot one last time and was killed when a wall collapsed on him.[175]

The day after this unfortunate incident, General Banks – not wanting more needless loss of life – ordered his men to leave the town. Military discipline was low in Banks' army at this point, but a new provost marshal, Lieutenant Colonel Bachelor, arrived to help restore military discipline. Kate Sperry remarked simply, "he is very polite."[176] This was quite a compliment coming from the staunch Confederate Kate Sperry.

---

[170] Ibid.
[171] Delauter, 36.
[172] Sperry, diary entry for June 12, 1862
[173] Ibid.
[174] Ibid.
[175] Delauter, 36.
[176] Sperry, diary entry for June 15, 1862

As the days passed, the town's besieged inhabitants went about their daily lives as best they could. Many of the town's women continued to make daily trips to the hospitals to give comfort to the sick and wounded soldiers, regardless of their uniform. Kate Sperry was one of those women and during one of her visits she took buttermilk and lemonade along. On arrival at the hospital, she handed the beverages to a Union officer who asked, "if it was poisoned?" Kate snapped back at him and "assured him it was."[177] Kate, of course, was only angry at the offensive question the officer asked.

Something of a controversy arose in the Union high command on June 27. General John C. Fremont and General Banks learned that Major General John Pope had been named commander of the Union's new Army of Virginia. Banks, although disgruntled at the news (he was senior to Pope), decided to accept the arrangement and obey orders. Fremont, however, was not so cool headed.

General Fremont was outraged at the choice and asked to be relieved of his duties. President Lincoln gratefully accepted the resignation, and General Franz Sigel, a German immigrant and one of the many political generals of the North, replaced Fremont. Fremont lacked military ability, as was illustrated by his disastrous defeat at Cross Keys on June 8, 1862. Still bitter over the

---

[177] Sperry, diary entry for June 23, 1862

command change in 1862, he attempted to run for president on a third party ticket that was comprised mainly of abolitionists and German-Americans in 1864.[178]   Fremont's second run for presidency did not turn out in his favor – he had run as the Republican candidate in 1856 – he withdrew from the presidential race on September 22, 1864.[179]

While the Union commanders bickered, beleaguered Winchester slowly adjusted to a different Federal commander, General Abraham Sanders Piatt.[180] He implemented strict policies and required people to take the oath of allegiance to the United States. Piatt's orders stipulated that any man who did not take the oath would be expelled from the town and would be killed if he returned.[181]

During the early days of Piatt's tenure, many of the blacks residing in town left their positions as servants and slaves and proclaimed their freedom. These "former" slaves were adamant about their rights to liberty and equality, and demanded wages for the services they provided their masters. The ardent, and obviously aggravated, secessionist Mr. Clark wrote:

> Large numbers of negros [sic] have left their homes
> within the past week, and the sentiment among
> them is universal that they are perfectly free and

---

[178] McPherson, 715.

[179] Ibid., 776. Fremont was the first Republican Party candidate for the presidency when he ran for the that office in 1856.

[180] Quarles, 80

[181] Ibid.

they seem to be more disposed than ever before to
avail themselves of their liberty. Some have gone
so far as to demand wages from their masters upon
condition of their remaining to work for them.[182]

Aside from enforcing his occupation policies, Piatt fortified the northwestern portion of Winchester. The main component of the new defensive works was Fort Garibaldi. The fort was obviously named after the 39th New York Infantry Regiment, better known as the Garibaldi Guard -- named in honor of the hero of Italian unification, Giuseppe Garibaldi -- whose soldiers aided in the construction of the fortification.[183] Numerous civilian-owned stonewalls and structures were dismantled to provide material for the fort's construction. The soldiers building the fort appeared to especially enjoy tearing down "Selma," the home of former United States Senator James Mason.[184] Many Northerners hated Mason even before secession because he had sponsored the Fugitive Slave Law into Congress.

On November 8, 1861, Mason and John Slidell were captured by the United States Navy while en route to Great Britain and France. The two men were Confederate Commissioners seeking foreign recognition and assistance for the Confederacy. The ship carrying the two men, the *Trent*, was a British mail ship, and when the *Trent's* captain refused to give up Mason and Slidell

---

[182] Clark, journal entry for June 30, 1861

[183] *O.R.* Ser I., Vol. XIX, Part 1, 533.

[184] Delauter, 38. It should also be mentioned here that Mason, during the war acted as a representative of the Confederate government to Great Britain, however, Great Britain never received him officially.

to the United States Navy two shots were fired across the ship's bow to force the captain to acquiesce.

This incident, tagged the "Trent Affair," temporarily created a warlike atmosphere between Great Britain and the United States. The British demanded the release of the men. President Lincoln feared that if he released the two it would be politically disastrous. Lincoln took the advice of his Secretary of State, William Seward, to release the men and avoid conflict with Great Britain. Seward used his political savvy in a letter to the British informing them of the release stating that he was happy to see that the British had finally followed the lead of the United States in recognizing the rights of neutral ships.

Back in Winchester, Piatt ordered all trees between the fort and the town cut down as part of the construction of Fort Garibaldi.[185] Clearing this field of fire heightened the citizens' fear that if the Confederate Army tried to reoccupy Winchester, the massive guns of the fort would fire on the town. Their fears increased when the fort's guns fired wooden practice rounds that landed in the streets on several occasions.[186]

Artillery practice aside, conditions worsened for the town's male citizenry on July 25, when General Pope issued orders to arrest any man refusing to swear allegiance to the United States.

---

[185] Quarles, 80.
[186] Ibid.

Several days later Piatt was relieved of his duties and the command of Winchester went to Brigadier General Julius White.[187]

General White was a marked contrast to his predecessor. He was better liked than Piatt and tried to be more accommodating to the citizens' needs. White initially halted artillery practice, but reconvened this noisy activity in early August. White, a former Wisconsin legislator, did not fully agree with the war and Pope's ill-considered edict regarding forced oaths of allegiance, but he obeyed his orders.

Even under White's lenient tenure, however, none of Winchester's residents were allowed any privileges unless they took the oath of allegiance. Reverend Brooke discovered this when he went to the local provost marshal's office to obtain a pass on August 15. Faced with this new requirement, Brooke held firm to his Confederate convictions and the fiery parson refused to take the oath.[188]

Five days after the Reverend's experience, he and a group of other citizens that included the mayor, were arrested and taken to General White's headquarters. Much to their surprise the meeting was extremely cordial. Reverend Brooke remembered: "I was arrested today with a number of citizens, by order of Gen.

---

[187] Ibid. There seems to be a degree of uncertainty about the exact date General Julius White became the post commander of Winchester. Garland Quarles uses the date of July 30, but Julia Chase in her diary notes that White replaced Piatt on June 26. Roger U. Delauter in his work on Winchester uses July 28, as the date of the command change.

[188] Brooke, journal entry for August 15, 1862. The entry reads: "Went to the Provost to get a pass – would not grant it unless we took the oath – we refused."

White… But they only took us to Headquarters where Gen. White gave the best dinner I have had since the war began."[189] Five days after this feast Brooke and the others were paroled.

As noted, White decided to recommence artillery practice at Fort Garibaldi in early August and the decision was nearly fatal for the Conner family. The morning air of August 18, was filled with the familiar smell of black powder and whizzing artillery shells, but during this round of practice a round went astray and crashed into the Conner home on Loudoun Street. Miraculously, none of the residents of the house were hurt or killed. Mrs. Lee recorded the incident and the good fortune of the Conner family in her diary:

> The first sound I heard yesterday morning was the rush of a cannon ball striking very near. I did not get up to see, but turned over to take my morning nap. It struck Conner's House on Loudoun Street, entered the side wall, passed through a passage, then into a chamber & through the beds usually occupied by the Conners & their little children. Providentially, they had gone to another room to sleep the night before & had intended occupying their own chamber the night the house was fired into, but for some reason they were prevented. Reed, our Mayor, wrote to Genl. White to remonstrate. He promised it should not be done again & apologized to the ladies of Winchester…Notwithstanding his promise they fired over the town again in the evening & again today.[190]

---

[189] Ibid., journal entry for August 20, 1862
[190] Lee, diary entry for August 19, 1862

Mr. Conner kept the artillery projectile for posterity and had it embedded into the wall of his home during the repairs.[191]

Several days later General White realized the military vulnerability of his position. On August 23, elements of the 12th Virginia Cavalry raided a train on the Winchester and Potomac Railroad, captured a handful of Union soldiers, and escaped with a fair amount of food.[192] White realized there were still many townspeople who refused the oath of allegiance and, with enemy forces in the area, believed his command was in jeopardy because citizens refusing to take the oath were free to provide aid to Rebel forces. To try to reduce the number of holdouts General White modified the oath. Although refusing to accept the modified oath, Mr. Clark recorded it in his journal:

> I,_____________, having been placed under arrest by
> the military authorities of the United States, with
> the liberty of the County of Frederick, Virginia, do
> solemnly swear that, until discharged from arrest, I
> will not take up arms against the United States nor
> perform any act, either overt or covert, prejudicial
> thereto, nor directly or indirectly furnish aid,
> comfort or information or allow any member of my
> family or any servant or employee to do so – and
> will report in person to the Provost Marshall at
> Winchester whenever required by him.[193]

After General Robert E. Lee's smashing victory over Pope at the Battle of Second Manassas on August 29-30, the Southern

---

[191] Delauter, 39, The home was demolished in 1959.
[192] Ibid.
[193] Clark, diary entry for September 1, 1862.

sympathizers of Winchester were strengthened in their beliefs. Lee won at Second Manassas on August 30, 1862, despite Union General Fitz John Porters' V Corps savage attack on Stonewall Jackson's line. Jackson held his ground stubbornly, however, and General James Longstreet's men shattered the Union attack as his men surged forward into the Union flank. After Second Manassas Lee pushed General Pope's right flank and another battle erupted at Chantilly on September 1, 1862, that ended in a stalemate. The victory at Manassas enabled Lee to move his triumphant yet bruised army across the Potomac River into Maryland. Lee did this to move the war out of Virginia and allow the Old Dominion's farmers time to harvest their crops. The Confederate commander also believed that thousands of Marylanders would join the Confederate service and that the United States government might possibly seek peace.[194] With the Confederates on the offensive, Winchester's citizens refused to take any form of the oath of allegiance to the Union.

The peaceful night of September 2, was shattered by shouting in the streets – a two-block section of the town was engulfed in flames.[195] As the fire raged, a shockwave like that from an earthquake rumbled through the town as White's rear guard blew up the magazine at Fort Garibaldi. General White had been ordered to take his force to Harpers Ferry to reinforce the

---

[194] For a complete study of Lee's strategy in 1862 see; Joseph L. Harsh, *Confederate Tide Rising: Robert E. Lee and the Making of Southern Strategy, 1861 – 1862* (Kent: The Kent State University Press, 1998).
[195] Clark., diary entry for September 8, 1862.

garrison there commanded by Colonel Dixon Miles.[196]   The movement to Harpers Ferry was prompted by the fear that General Lee's force, after crushing Pope at Chantilly on September 1, might move into the Shenandoah Valley and capture White. "Last night, the magazine… was blown up and General White left with 10,000 men", remembered Reverend Brooke in his journal.[197]

When the citizens awoke the next morning, the despised Union soldiers had departed. Kate Sperry wrote of the withdrawal:

> Winchester is once more free from Yankees… It
> seems that the Yanks hadn't the slightest idea of
> leaving before dark and received orders to evacuate
> in the night… They then set fire to a large quantity
> of provender and blew up the magazine… Only
> about one company of our men came in Winchester
> this morning![198]

During the morning following the Union Army's evacuation, Lieutenant Colonel John H.S. Funk arrived in Winchester with the 5th Virginia Infantry.[199] General White had destroyed a large portion of Union supplies, but many items were salvageable. Funk's men gathered shoes, ammunition, guns, tents, cooking utensils, and other useful items. Aside from Winchester's handful of Unionists, the townspeople's morale was lifted by the

---

[196] *O.R.*, Ser. I, Vol. XII, Part 2, 767.
[197] Brooke, journal entry for September 3, 1862
[198] Sperry, diary entry for September 3, 1862
[199] *O.R.,* Ser. I, Vol. XIX, Part 1, 139.

change of garrisons. "The whole community felt an immense load had been taken from them", remembered a delighted Mr. Clark.[200]

General Lee initiated his first invasion of the North as Confederate units crossed the Potomac River at White's Ford near Leesburg into Maryland. Lee was putting into play the strategy that he devised after Second Manassas. In this strategy, General Lee had a vital purpose in mind for Winchester. The town's role in the Maryland Campaign was crucial as it served as a depot for the Army of Northern Virginia and equipment of all sorts was stored in its warehouses.[201] A facility for repairing artillery pieces also was established in the town.

As Lee pressed into Maryland, incapacitated soldiers were sent back to Winchester for care and treatment. The town continued its customary role as a safe haven for afflicted soldiers and the citizens once again cared for the casualties.

Lee's Maryland Campaign culminated in the Battle of Antietam near the town of Sharpsburg on September 17. The battle, now remembered as the "Bloodiest Day in American History," lasted about twelve hours and ended in a general stalemate. Lee's first attempt at an invasion of the North had failed. The draw at Sharpsburg was the closest the Union Army in the east had come to victory and it gave President Lincoln the political opportunity he needed to issue the preliminary

---

[200] Clark, diary entry for September 8, 1862
[201] *O.R.*, Ser. I, Vol. XIX, Part 1, 139.

Emancipation Proclamation; the actual Proclamation did not become effective until January 1, 1863.

After the Battle of Antietam, Winchester was again transformed into a vast military hospital. Even though the inhabitants were accustomed to such scenes, the results of each battle were still heart wrenching. Only limited indoor space was available for the thousands of casualties and many wounded men were strewn about in the open as they waited for attention.[202] For some of the sick and wounded, no attention was available and they died alone.

The Confederate Army camped north of town near Bunker Hill after the Battle of Antietam. The close proximity of the army to town allowed many Confederate officers and men to make social visits to Winchester. The first liberator of the town, "Stonewall" Jackson, made several social appearances. As expected, he attended services at the Kent Street Presbyterian Church, but aside from his spiritual obligations, Jackson also made some uncharacteristic social calls. On October 28, he visited the North Cameron Street home of Mrs. Lee. Dr. Hunter McGuire, a Winchester native and Jackson's medical director, accompanied Jackson on the visit and as he and his commander approached the home, Mrs. Lee was on her front porch. Mrs. Lee recorded her thoughts as the two approached: "I saw Hunter McGuire approaching with a plain-looking officer, whom I did not

---

[202] Robertson, *Stonewall Jackson: The Man, The Soldier, The Legend,* 625.

recognize; imagine my delight when he introduced General Jackson."[203]

While Jackson was at the Lee home, he listened intently as Mrs. Lee told him of the harshness of the Union occupiers. After several hours of conversation, he bade farewell to her and proceeded to the home of Dr. McGuire's parents for dinner.[204] During the dinner, Dr. McGuire's sister, Marguerita, asked Jackson if he would have his photograph taken for her and much to everyone's surprise Jackson agreed.

The crooked button photograph of Jackson taken by Nathaniel Routzahn. This is only one of two photographs taken of Jackson during the war. The other photograph was taken several weeks prior to his death. The townspeople of Winchester were deeply saddened by the death of the "Mighty Stonewall". (Winchester-Frederick County Historical Society)

---

[203] Lee, diary entry for October 28, 1862.
[204] Delauter, 43.

After Jackson excused himself from the dinner table, he went directly to the studio of Nathaniel Routzahn. Accompanied by Reverend Graham, the two men strolled several blocks down Loudoun Street to the studio where Jackson seated himself in front of the camera. The photographer noticed that the General was missing a button on his uniform coat. Jackson cared little about formality, but he took a needle and thread, and personally sewed the button back on the coat. Unfortunately he sewed it on crooked. The image in this crooked-button photograph became Mary Anna's favorite likeness of her husband.[205]

This cheerfulness was soon dampened by the sight of elements of General James Longstreet's Corps marching south through Winchester toward Culpeper Court House. The Army of the Potomac was on the move and Lee had to move his forces to counter the emerging threat. Jackson's corps remained to protect the Winchester area. This, of course, pleased many people in Winchester and in the weeks that followed Longstreet's withdrawal Jackson masterfully kept the Union forces at bay by constantly maneuvering in and out of nearby Berkeley, Jefferson, Frederick, and Clarke counties.[206]

By mid-November 1862, Major General Ambrose Burnside had replaced McClellan as the commander of the Army of the Potomac and was moving toward the Rappahannock River and

---

[205] Robertson, *Stonewall Jackson: The Man, The Soldier, The Legend*, 638. On this page Robertson recounts the story of the photograph.
[206] Delauter, 42.

Fredericksburg, Virginia. Lee needed to concentrate his corps and ordered Jackson to move to Fredericksburg with all possible haste. As Jackson departed Mrs. Lee's home on October 28, she remarked she wished he could stay in Winchester for the winter. Jackson expressed the same sentiment, but duty beckoned and on November 22, Mrs. Lee's hopes departed along with Jackson's corps.[207] This was the last time the inhabitants of Winchester saw their hero Jackson.[208]

Only a token Confederate force remained after Jackson's departure. The defense of Winchester was left to a small brigade of cavalry commanded by Brigadier General William "Grumble" Jones and the men of the Maryland Line under Brigadier General George H. Steuart.[209] The townspeople were disheartened to see Jackson and so many Valley men depart, but were delighted to remain under Confederate protection. Kate Sperry wrote: "I am glad they are going to leave a force here, for I dread the Yanks more than ever."[210]

Unfortunately for Kate Sperry and her Confederate neighbors, the Federals wasted no time reoccupying Winchester. During the early hours of December 2, a Union force of 3,000 soldiers under the command of General John Geary departed

---

[207] Lee, diary entry for October 28, 1862.

[208] Jackson never returned to Winchester after November 22, 1862. He died on May 10, 1863.

[209] Robert J. Driver Jr., *First and Second Maryland Cavalry, C.S.A.* (Charlottesville, Va.: Rockbridge Publishing, 1999), 27; Delauter, 45.

[210] Sperry, diary entry for November 20, 1862.

Harpers Ferry for Winchester.[211] The following morning, Geary proceeded cautiously to Winchester; as his force approached the Confederate defenders began to withdraw. Geary's troops took position on rising ground immediately east of Winchester and prepared for battle.[212]

While forming his lines, Geary was approached by a number of civilians who informed him that the Confederate forces of Jones and Steuart had left the previous night. For the most part this was true; only small pockets of troops and incapacitated soldiers remained. Armed with this knowledge, Geary sent a message to the mayor, J.B.T. Reed, under a flag of truce.[213]

Dr. A.M. Ball, the medical director of the division, Captain R.C. Shannon assistant-adjutant general of the Second Brigade, and an orderly carried Geary's message into town.[214] In the message, General Geary asked Mayor Reed to surrender the town unconditionally. If Winchester surrendered, Geary promised to respect the inhabitants and their property, but if Reed failed to comply Geary was prepared to take the town with whatever force necessary.[215]

Geary received a response from Major Samuel B. Myers of the 7th Virginia Cavalry requesting a respite of one hour to allow

---

[211] Delauter, 45.
[212] *O.R.,* Ser, I, Vol. XXI, 33.
[213] *O.R.* Ser. I, Vol. XXI, 33.
[214] Ibid.
[215] Ibid.

remaining Confederate soldiers and non-combatants to depart. Major Myers message read:

> General: The city of Winchester will be evacuated in an hour's [sic] time by the military fordes under my command, which time I would request for you to be pleased to observe, to give non-combatants desirous of leaving the town an opportunity to do so. I have the honor to be, general, your obedient servant.[216]

Geary refused Major Myers request and in his report of the action wrote: "I peremptorily refused the demand of an hour's time for non-combatants to depart."[217] Union forces took position north of town in fortifications previously constructed.[218] As Geary's artillery rolled into these defensive works they spotted a small body of enemy cavalry. Federal artillery shortly commenced fire on the unit and dispersed it. A disappointed Kate Sperry recorded the episode:

> …they sent in a flag of truce about 12 O'clock… after which their army, about 4 or 5,000… passed across the upper end of town to the fortifications from whence they could see our pickets on the adjoining hill a mile off so they began firing on them and a few of the infantry straggled through the street and about 39 of the cavalry.[219]

After Winchester was occupied, Geary learned of a large number of smallpox cases in the town. Instead of risking

---

[216] Ibid.
[217] Ibid.
[218] Ibid.
[219] Sperry, diary entry for December 5, 1862.

additional infections, he held the main element of the Union force north of town while a small unit entered and searched the town. This search yielded 118 Confederates, including four officers, and by 3 p.m. these prisoners were paroled and Geary withdrew his force to Harpers Ferry.[220] Kate Sperry counted her blessings as Geary departed:

> Thank goodness the Yanks have left bag and baggage… the cause of their abrupt departure is supposed to be that they were afraid to stay or found that they could gain nothing by staying here so after taking possession and paroling all the sick at the hospital away they went.[221]

In Geary's report of this operation, he noted that when his troops entered town they encountered Union sympathizers who greeted the Federals with symbols of the United States.[222]

After Geary withdrew, "Grumble" Jones returned once more with his Confederate force.[223] Jones remained in Winchester until December 13, but he withdrew his command to Strasburg.[224] In the week and a half that followed, Winchester enjoyed a peaceful, unoccupied tranquillity. This serenity ended abruptly in the early morning hours of December 23, with the unexpected arrival of Union cavalry. These widely despised Federal troopers remained for only a few hours before departing, however.

---

[220] *O.R.,* Ser. I, Vol. XXI, 33.
[221] Sperry, diary entry for December 5, 1862.
[222] *O.R.,* Ser. I, Vol. XXI, 34.
[223] Driver, 27.
[224] Delauter, 46.

The following day, Christmas Eve, marked the beginning of another lengthy Union occupation.   A new force of about 3,000 entered the town and Union soldiers set up camp on the property of the colonial founder of Winchester, James Wood.[225]

This force was commanded by Brigadier General Gustave Paul Cluseret, a native of France who came to America in 1862 to fight for the Union. Cluseret was an experienced military officer, having served in the French military. He left the French Army in 1858 for New York where he worked as a banker, but returned to Europe in 1860 to fight for Italian liberation. Despite the fact that Cluseret came to the United States to fight for the Union he did not hold the radical ideologies of some of his superiors. As a result, Cluseret clashed with Brigadier General Robert H. Milroy in January 1863 and soon resigned. Cluseret was not a proponent of emancipation and saw no point in being harsh to the Confederate civilian population. Mrs. Lee wrote: "…he [Cluseret] did not come here to fight for negroes [sic], & to arrest women, & [believed] that it is contrary to the usages of war, to refuse to feed prisoners."[226] While in Winchester, Cluseret implemented a 7:00 p.m. curfew and threatened to arrest anyone out after that time. On Christmas Day, he ordered the search of homes.[227] The Union soldiers performed these searches regularly, but it was not his intention to destroy civilian property; in a number of instances,

---

[225] Gwin, ed., 102; Delauter, 46.
[226] Lee, diary entry for January 10, 1863.
[227] Delauter, 46.

Cluseret prevented acts of destruction and posted armed guards at the homes of victimized citizens to prevent additional violence.[228]

During the final days of 1862, Winchester's Confederate citizens believed they were once again under the yoke of Federal oppression. The battles and harsh occupations the citizens endured during the opening years of the war, however, had not prepared them for the coming harsh winter under Federal control. Indeed, nothing could have prepared them for the next several dreadful months.

---

[228] Gwin, ed., 106. For more information on General Cluseret see Lowell L. Blaisdell, "A French Civil War Adventurer: Fact and Fancy" *Civil War History: A Journal of the Middle Period* (Vol. XII, 1966), 246-57: Philip M. Katz, *From Appomattox to Montmartre: Americans and the Paris Commune* (Cambridge: Harvard University Press, 1998).

The New Year brought the man who came to be arguably the most despised Union commander who controlled Winchester during the war, General Robert H. Milroy. Milroy's harsh treatment of the civilian population made many Confederates compare him to Union Major General Benjamin Butler. Milroy, however, treated the civilians of Winchester more callous than "Beast" Butler ever treated the inhabitants of New Orleans.[229] The policies Milroy implemented demonstrated his position as a strong advocate of Lincoln's Emancipation Proclamation and his harsh edicts led Virginia's Governor Letcher to brand him a war criminal.[230]

Milroy's force at Winchester was part of Major General Robert Schenck's Middle Department. From his position at Winchester, Milroy was able to deploy detachments to contend with Confederate raiders threatening the Baltimore and Ohio Railroad, while the fortifications around Winchester protected his

---

[229] It must be noted that Union General Benjamin Butler, upon arrival in New Orleans on May 1, 1862 did not intend to punish that city's inhabitants. Butler did not withhold the necessaries of life from those who refused the oath of allegiance, nor did Butler arrest or exile women for insulting Union soldiers. For more on Butler's occupation of New Orleans see: Chester G. Hearn, *When the Devil Came Down to Dixie: Ben Butler in New Orleans* (Baton Rouge: Louisiana State University Press, 1997).

[230] Edward H. Philips, *The Lower Shenandoah Valley in the Civil War: The Impact of War Upon the Civilian Population and Upon Civilian Institutions* (Lynchburg, Va.: H.E. Howard, 1993), 154.

command on three sides. In the town, Portia Baldwin Baker, a woman in her mid-twenties, described the actions of the Federal soldiers thusly:

> They are foot by foot and plank by plank destroying our property. They give us no privileges. God tender their hearts. I can pray for them but I don't know how to pass them, without wishing bad things. I can love them so much more when they are far off. I am always wishing them in their homes.[231]

Military rule prior to Milroy's arrival paled before his harsh decrees and the punishment his soldiers inflicted for any infraction of his rules. Milroy's rules and regulations are too numerous to list, but some of the most unpopular deserve recognition. For example, if any citizen, man or woman, insulted a Union soldier in any way punishment was rendered.[232] The penalty for such an insult was usually imprisonment.[233] Milroy also prohibited the sale of produce in town by any outside farmer; this act of food denial infuriated the townspeople. He also prevented any sutler from selling goods to any resident who had not taken the oath of allegiance to the United States or possessed a permit from the

---

[231] Portia Baldwin Baker, "Diary, Sept. 19, 1859 – Jan. 8, 1863" 1178 WFCHS, Archives Room, Handley Regional Library, Winchester, VA, diary entry for New Year's Day, 1863.

[232] Delauter, 47.

[233] Lee, diary entry for January 2, 1863. In her diary Mrs. Lee writes: "…if his men are insulted by word or manner, by male or female, they shall be imprisoned."

provost marshal's office to make purchases.[234] The fiery Mrs. Lee remarked: "Milroy is trying to starve us out."[235] Winchester's citizens, however, found ways to beat Milroy's rules and get food. Mrs. Lee usually sent out requests to friends in Baltimore for supplies and had friends in town with permits purchase goods for her from the sutlers. Others received their supplies from sympathetic Union soldiers.[236] Milroy prohibited communication between the inhabitants of the town and those residing outside the town limits, and the mood in town became tense as even groups of schoolgirls were dispersed if they gathered in a group of two or more.[237]

Like General Piatt before him, Milroy rewarded the taking of the oath of allegiance with privileges that made a citizen's life easier. He believed that withholding necessities from individuals refusing to take the oath might eventually force them to do so. While this method was intended to increase Union sentiment in the area, other Union officers including General Cluseret disagreed with Milroy and thought this policy would do the exact opposite.[238]

---

[234] Special Order No. 4, (Special Orders. Apr. 1862 – June 1863, RG 393, Vol. II, National Archives and Records Administration).

[235] Lee, diary entry for January 10, 1863.

[236] Ibid., diary entries for the months of February and March 1863; Gwin, ed. 123, 129.

[237] Gwin, ed. 123.

[238] Cary C. Collins, "Grey Eagle: Major General Robert Huston Milroy and the Civil War" *Indiana Magazine of History* (March 1994), 65.

Kate Sperry and a friend once visited Milroy's headquarters. Sperry's friend's baggage had been confiscated and she wanted it returned. The two women pleaded with him for the baggage. Milroy was rude to both women and told them that unless they took the oath of allegiance the luggage would not be returned. Kate and her friend did not accept Milroy's demand and went away empty handed, but with their pride. Sperry recalled the confrontation:

> We went to Milroy's head – quarters nearly opposite the Court House and saw the old villain. He told her she could get her things if she took the oath and as she wouldn't he just waived [sic] her out of the room. He's a second Butler and $100,000 is the price the Confederacy (some people in the Confederacy) has placed on his head – I wish I could get it.[239]

Milroy had no sympathy for these women, or any other woman in Winchester or the Confederacy. He believed that if it had not been for the Southern women, the men in the Confederate Army would have quit fighting long ago.

Mrs. Lee had no regard for Milroy, a man she thought a tyrant, but she still had to abide by his rules for her own safety. Like a schoolgirl asking her parents' permission for a friend stay the night, she went to the provost's office to obtain approval for the Sherrards to spend the night at her home. The Sherrards were

---

[239] Sperry, diary entry for January 21, 1863. In her recollections, she is referring to General Benjamin F. Butler, a man who was viewed as a tyrant when he served as military governor of New Orleans.

one of Winchester's prominent families and Mrs. Lee's closest friends. Mr. Joseph Sherrard was cashier of the Farmer's Bank of Virginia and later became a judge.[240] Mrs. Lee did not meet Milroy personally, as only a soldier was in the provost office, but the enlisted man was sympathetic and granted her request without insisting she take the oath of allegiance. She wrote of the visit: "Then with Jeannie Sherrard to the Provost Marshals to see if the Sherrards might be allowed the privilege of staying with us… the permission was graciously accorded by our tyrant."[241]

News of Milroy's harsh practices spread quickly and his actions prompted General Lee to take action. Lee ordered Brigadier General John Imboden to do whatever he could to stop Milroy's demeaning rules. Furthermore, Lee recommended that the Secretary of War, James A. Seddon, order all prisoners taken from Milroy's command be held as hostages to ensure the safety of Winchester's citizens. Lee also wrote to Union General-in-Chief Halleck addressing Milroy's treatment of the inhabitants of the region. Halleck responded to Lee's letter and informed him that after investigation if the policies were found unauthorized, Milroy would be ordered to conform to United States Army regulations.[242]

---

[240] Quarles, 28.

[241] Lee, diary entry for January 7, 1863.

[242] Douglas Southall Freeman, ed., *Lee's Dispatches: Unpublished Letters of General Robert E. Lee, C.S.A., To Jefferson Davis And The War Department Of The Confederate States of America 1862 – 1865* (Baton Rouge: Louisiana State University Press, 1957), 71.

While policing the local population, Milroy fortified the northern portion of the town with two new defensive works. He rebuilt Fort Garibaldi; afterwards it was referred to as Fort Milroy or Flag Fort. The other major work constructed was Star Fort, which was built on the old site of Fort Alabama, a series of gun emplacements built by Jackson earlier in the war.[243] In June 1863, Star Fort held four twenty-pound Parrott rifles, two twenty-four pound mountain howitzers, and could hold a garrison of more than 2,000 men.[244] As the days passed, Milroy's force also increased and by early March his command consisted of two infantry brigades, three regiments of cavalry, and three artillery batteries.

Shortly after his arrival, Milroy established his headquarters in the home of Mrs. Logan at the corner of Braddock and Piccadilly Streets. Like General Hatch, he allowed the Logans to reside in a small portion of their house. In early April, Mrs. Milroy joined her husband. Her arrival unleashed a chain of events that severed the already tenuous connection between the townspeople and Milroy. After his wife arrived, the Milroys evicted the Logans from their home and Winchester. One of Mrs. Logan's daughters had erysipelas and the child was not allowed to take medicine with her.[245] Mrs. Lee, outraged as were many of the inhabitants, wrote: "They are not allowed to have a trunk or to

---

[243] Robert M. Rhodes, "Our Forts", *The Story of Frederick County* (Winchester: 1989), 33.
[244] Beck & Grunder, *The Second Battle of Winchester*, 15.
[245] Lee, diary entry for April 7, 1863. Erysipelas is a type of severe skin infection.

be alone long enough to change their dresses, sentinals [sic] watching every movement…"[246] Kate Sperry, upset by this brutal treatment wrote:

> Today the Yanks sent away Mr. Logan's whole family – three daughters, two sons, and his wife… All of Mr. Logan's and his sons' clothing was confiscated, together with the house and furniture, besides a large supply of provisions, for the use of Mrs. Gen. Milroy, who sat in an ambulance and viewed their removal with the utmost complacency.[247]

In Milroy's eyes, this cold-hearted act was taken as retaliation for the ill treatment of a Jessie Scout – a unit of Union soldiers posing as Confederate troops – by the Logans on the morning of April 6. The act was in keeping with his policy to punish anyone who mistreated Union soldiers. Mrs. Lee, in her diary recorded the treatment of the Jessie Scout: "They collared him, shook him, and threw him out of the house."[248]

As the Logans sat in an ambulance that was to carry them south past the Union line to Newtown, Mrs. Milroy stood at the front door of her new home. In an angry rage, May Logan, one of Mrs. Logan's three daughters pointed her finger at a Union soldier and yelled, "There is a man whose brains I could blow out."[249]

---

[246] Ibid.
[247] Sperry, diary entry for April 7, 1863.
[248] Lee, diary entry for April 6, 1863.
[249] Ibid., diary entry for April 7, 1863.

The eviction of the Logan family not only unleashed additional hatred for Milroy in Winchester, but this was viewed with disapproval by some of his own subordinates. Other Federal officers boarding at the Logan home were furious over the treatment of the family and threatened to resign their commissions.[250] The Union officer escorting the Logans beyond the Union lines expressed his deepest sympathy to the family and for expressing his sympathy he was dishonorably discharged from the service by Milroy.[251] There is no doubt that some dissension occurred in the Union ranks and Mrs. Lee remarked: "… it is said that six officers have resigned in consequence & that even the privates are indignant at the outrage."[252] The aftermath of the Logan affair began to resemble a mutiny. One of the officers who boarded at the home, for example, reportedly tore off his shoulder boards and threw them at Milroy's feet.[253]

A month after the Logan family was exiled devastating news arrived from eastern Virginia – Stonewall Jackson was dead. During the Battle of Chancellorsville, on the evening of May 2, 1863, Jackson and his staff had gone out to reconnoiter the Federal line, and upon returning to the Confederate position a North

---

[250] Sperry, diary entry for April 7, 1863.

[251] Lee, diary entry for April 9, 1863.

[252] Ibid.

[253] Gettie [Margaretta] Miller, "Diary, march 23, 1862 – Sept. 9, 1863", 301 WFCHS – Godfrey Miller Collection, Archives Room, Handley Regional Library, Winchester, VA, diary entry for April 8, 1863. The complete entry reads: "They say that some of the yankees officers resigned their office and that the one that boarded at Mrs. Logan's tore off his shoulder straps and thru [sic] them down at old Milroy's feet and he had been courtmarshaled [sic]."

General Robert H. Milroy educated at Captain Partridge's Academy in Norwich, Vermont, served in the Mexican War and when the Civil War broke out became colonel of the 9th Indiana Infantry. Despite his possible mental instability during the Battle of Second Manassas, Milroy received his commission to major general in November 1862, however official word of his commission did not reach him in Winchester until March 1863. Without a doubt, Milroy was the most despised Union general to ever set foot in Winchester. After a court of inquiry exonerated him for his defeat at the Second Battle of Winchester he was sent to Tennessee. After the Civil War he became an Indian agent in Olympia, Washington. He died in 1890.(Robert H. Milroy Collection, Jasper County Public Library, Indiana)

Carolina regiment mistakenly fired at Jackson and his staff. Jackson was struck three times – his left arm was later amputated and for the next several days appeared to be healing. His condition, however, took a turn for the worst and he perished on May 10, 1863, from the complications of pneumonia. The women of Winchester showed their love for Jackson by adorning themselves with mourning ribbons that had a Virginia seal in the center.[254] These badges created some controversy and the women had to remove the Virginia state seal button because Milroy recognized the seal as a Confedederate symbol and under Milroy's reign it was illegal to possess such symbols. Milroy ordered that the women replace the Virginia seal with an image of George Washington. A heart-broken Mrs. Lee, no doubt recalling Jackson's visit to her home, wrote:

> … the American says the Richmond papers obtain the obituary of Genl. Jackson. I do not believe it yet, though the bare idea has given me a more hopeless feeling than any other event of the war. Not that I despair at the final result, but it would be as if God were for awhile leaving us to grope in the dark – in depriving us of one of His purest saints.[255]

Confederate supporters had a great affection for Jackson and there was probably no town in the Confederacy that had a greater affinity for Jackson than Winchester. Jackson, while away in the saddle, seemed to keep the Valley town in his heart. His belief in "Yankee barbarity" surely was sharpened by the Union soldiers' treatment of Mrs. Logan and their cursing at school children. Kate Sperry, whose father had served in Jackson's command, expressed her sorrow with a heavy heart at the news of his death:

---

[254] Delauter, 50.
[255] Lee, diary entry for May 13, 1863.

> I firmly believe he's dead (Jackson) and feel so miserable – nearly cried my eyes out – poor Jackson – so noble – so brave – so loved by all the people – Oh, how we shall miss him. We've never had one to fill Ashby's place, and although I know we've other good generals, yet they arn't [sic] Jackson – I don't like seeing our soldiers unless he is at their head – I was so thankful when I heard his left arm was amputated, but that he was doing well. I was so very thankful he wasn't killed, and now to hear he is dead is too bad – though, as he said when his arm was amputated. "It is all right or the Lord would not have ordered it so." There was no more pleasure for me after that dreadful news.[256]

General Lee again seized the strategic initiative after defeating Union General Joseph Hooker at Chancellorsville on May 4.[257] The gateway for Lee's invasion into Pennsylvania was the Shenandoah Valley and only Winchester's Union garrison stood between the Army of Northern Virginia and the Potomac River at the edge of the North's heartland.

While Milroy's garrison rested comfortably at Winchester, Lee set his invasion plans into motion. General Richard S. Ewell, commanding Lee's Second Corps, spearheaded the army's advance west of the Blue Ridge Mountains. He knew the area well from campaigning with Jackson and was ordered to proceed to Winchester, dislodge Milroy, and then move across the Potomac.

---

[256] Sperry, diary entry for May 13, 1863.

[257] The Battle of Chancellorsville took place from May 2-4, 1863. On May 4, the advance of Major General John Sedgwick's command was halted, and on May 6 General Hooker withdrew.

The Stonewall Brigade proudly led the Confederate column toward Winchester when Ewell's corps departed Culpeper Court House on June 10. The men's excitement increased as they moved closer to their home region, a place they had not seen since the previous November. On June 12, Ewell's corps was positioned only twenty miles from Winchester. The next morning, and following the successful strategy previously employed at Winchester by Jackson, Ewell split his forces. Half his command, under Major General Edward Johnson was sent forward on the Front Royal Pike and approached Winchester from the southeast, while General Jubal Early's division made its way on the Valley Pike to approach the town from the south. General Robert Rodes' division was deployed to the east to trap the Federals at Berryville before marching to Martinsburg to cut off a Union retreat from Winchester.[258]

In early June, Milroy's was deeply worried by the possibility that Lee was going to attack Winchester. No doubt overjoyed at the possibility of seeing the friendly faces of the Confederate Army, Mrs. Lee noted: "The Federals are in a panic."[259] Milroy's force had every reason for worry given their skirmishes in May and the defeat of Hooker at Chancellorsville; the Confederate threat appeared overwhelming. After weeks of

---

[258] Beck & Grunder, *The Second Battle of Winchester*, 23-4; Delauter, 51, Freeman, *R.E. Lee*, 3:33. This endnote covers the entire paragraph.
[259] Lee, diary entry for June 5, 1863.

alerts and warnings, Milroy became complacent in the Winchester defenses.

Late on June 11, Milroy received orders to join General Benjamin Kelley at Harpers Ferry, but Milroy was buoyed by a false sense of security and ensured his superiors that he could easily hold Winchester. The first evidence of Ewell's movement to Winchester appeared at Middletown, south of Winchester, on June 12. While a minor skirmish by Civil War standards, Confederate forces under Captain W.L. Rasin, 1st Maryland Infantry, were forced to retreat after a skirmish with elements of the 87th Pennsylvania Infantry, 13th Pennsylvania Cavalry, and the 5th U.S. Artillery.[260] Milroy's confidence was boosted when these troops returned to Winchester with news of their victory.

The victory at Middletown made Milroy even more certain that he could stay and defend Winchester successfully. General Henry Halleck ordered Milroy to pull back to Harpers Ferry on June 11, but Milroy remained at Winchester.[261] Ignoring Halleck's repeated orders to pull back to the relative safety at Harpers Ferry, Milroy remained in Winchester and prepared to fight. Milroy would soon wish that he had followed "Old Brains" Halleck's orders.

---

[260] Beck and Grunder, *The Second Battle of Winchester*, 25.
[261] Roy Basler, ed. *The Collected Works of Abraham Lincoln* (New Brunswick: Rutgers University Press, 1953), 6:308.

Milroy's decision to defy Halleck and hold his position was based on the following reasons: first, Winchester was critical to keeping the Baltimore and Ohio Railroad open; second, the fortifications around Winchester were meant to withstand a force five times greater than his own (or so Milroy believed); third, there were a number of strong supporters of the Union in the area and he did not want to abandon them; and, finally, he did not want the Confederate forces to acquire the crops to be harvested in the area.[262]

On June 13, the crackle of musketry filled the air around noon as skirmishers from the 2nd Virginia Infantry engaged Union pickets positioned south of town. The Virginians drove the pickets back and advanced to high ground at the intersection of the Front Royal Pike and Millwood Pike before pressing on past Hollingsworth's Mill.[263] As the roar of musketry and artillery intensified so did the townspeople's curiosity. Excited and disregarding personal safety, they climbed to their rooftops for a glimpse of the soldiers in gray who came to deliver them from Milroy's tyranny.

As the citizens peered into the direction of the sound of battle, Major General Edward "Old Allegheny" Johnson's division

---

[262] *O.R.,* Ser. I, Vol. XXVIII, Part 2, 178.
[263] Beck and Grunder, *The Second Battle of Winchester*, 29.

advanced on the Front Royal Pike and converged with Major General Jubal Early, whose troops came up the Valley Pike. General Early arrived at Kernstown, formed his division into line of battle, and moved across the field where Stonewall Jackson met defeat, to attack Pritchard's Hill. This piece of high ground was essential because it commanded the Valley Pike south of town.

Four Union regiments were positioned on Pritchard's Hill along with two artillery pieces.[264] The Union force resisted Early's assault for some time, but Early struck repeatedly at the right flank of the Union line until the line cracked. Early, after rolling up the right flank, pushed only as far as Cedar Creek Grade where he was halted by Union forces. Johnson's division pressed to the intersection of the Front Royal and Millwood Pikes while Early rested his troops less than one mile south of town.[265]

Heavy rain on the night of June 13, did not slow Union activity in Winchester. The town bustled with activity as Milroy's garrison rushed about to prepare the place's defenses. With animals, wagons, and men dashing about the streets all night, Mrs. Lee was unable to sleep and wrote in her diary:

---

[264] Ibid.
[265] Delauter, 52.

> The Cavalry, Artillery & wagons were dashing about all nigh[t]; Milroy says they are fighting at Millwood & White Post… the Yankees say they worsted us in a skirmish last evening & that they have brought in 30 prisoners… They are packing up at the Commissaries. I have everything in nice order for the Confederates.[266]

Confident that his men could stave off an attack on their fortifications, Milroy ordered his command to withdraw into the town's three main fortifications: Flag Fort (Fort Milroy), West Fort, and Star Fort. Milroy had no communications with Washington, D.C. – the Confederates cut the telegraph lines – and so Milroy never received the telegram from General Schenck ordering him to hold Winchester.[267] Milroy spent June 14, in the fortifications with his binoculars, searching for any aggressive movements by General Ewell's forces. A staff officer noted of Milroy's vigilance: "All day, under the burning sun did General Milroy keep his position in the lookout, and with a glass anxiously scan the surrounding country."[268]

In mid-morning Milroy received the first indication of Ewell's intentions when musket fire erupted in the streets. Two Confederate regiments had pushed back a token Union force, occupied Bowers Hill, and entered the town. Throughout the day small skirmishes erupted, but they were only a prelude to a grand assault. The men firing in the streets had been from Early's

---

[266] Lee, diary entry for June 13, 1863.
[267] Collins, 66.
[268] *O.R.* Ser. I, Vol. XXVII, Part 2, 55.

division, but to avoid civilian casualties, he ordered the men out of town.

In the First Battle of Winchester, the high ground to the west of town was the key to the battle. While the location of the fighting was different, a flanking maneuver to the west would again defeat the fortified Federals. When Ewell and Early met atop Bowers Hill they planned the assault intended to crush Milroy's fortified line.

Ewell's plan was masterful. He placed General John Brown Gordon's brigade, the Maryland Line, and two batteries on Bowers Hill, then ordered Early to march west before turning north to position himself to strike Milroy at West Fort.[269] The success of Early's ten-mile march and subsequent attack on West Fort was the key to a Confederate victory. He moved his command from Bowers Hill and then circled around to the southeast before proceeding north across Cedar Creek Grade where he directed his division north across the Romney Road and halted it between the Romney and Pughtown Roads on the west side of West Fort. Milroy recognized the immediate threat to West Fort and reinforced it with infantry and two guns from the 5th U.S. Artillery.[270]

By 5 p.m., Early completed his march and placed twenty guns on the reverse slope of the ridge west of West Fort. Although the Union troops in the fort – the 110th Ohio Volunteer Infantry,

---

[269] Beck and Grunder, *Second Battle of Winchester*, 35.
[270] Ibid.

one company of the 116th Ohio Volunteer Infantry and six guns – had already received fire from Bowers Hill earlier they remained calm and at 5 p.m. prepared a soldier's supper of coffee, soup, and bread.[271]

Approximately one hour after Early placed his troops into position, his guns opened on West Fort.[272] Brigadier General Harry T. Hays' Louisiana Brigade was ordered to spearhead the assault. Hays' brigade consisted of five regiments, but as the forty-five minute artillery barrage continued, the Louisiana soldiers positioned at the end of a wood-line were subject to fire from heavy Union guns and deadly fire of Henry repeating rifles in the hands of crack riflemen.[273] While Hays' brigade did not suffer too many casualties from this sustained fire, it made the assault elements uneasy.

Hays sent word to Early that the assault had to start immediately. Early agreed. Hays placed three regiments in front, two in rear, and ordered them to attack. Slightly over a year had

---

[271] Beck and Grunder, *The Second Battle of Winchester*, 80. In reference to the regimental and artillery strength. Terry L. Jones, "Going Back Into The Union At Last, A Louisiana Tiger's account of the Gettysburg Campaign" *Civil War Times Illustrated* (January/February 1991), 55.

[272] Terry L. Jones, ed. *The Civil War Memoirs of Captain William J. Seymour: Reminiscences of a Louisiana Tiger* (Baton Rouge: Louisiana State University Press, 1991), 61.

[273] Beck and Grunder, *Second Battle of Winchester*, 41; in reference to the Union troops being armed with Henry Rifles. John D. McAulay, *Civil War Breechloading Rifles, A Survey of the Innovative Infantry Arms of the American Civil War* (Lincoln,R.I.: Andrew Mowbrey Inc., 1993), 42; The Henry Repeating Rifle's magazine located underneath the barrel had the capacity to hold fifteen rounds.

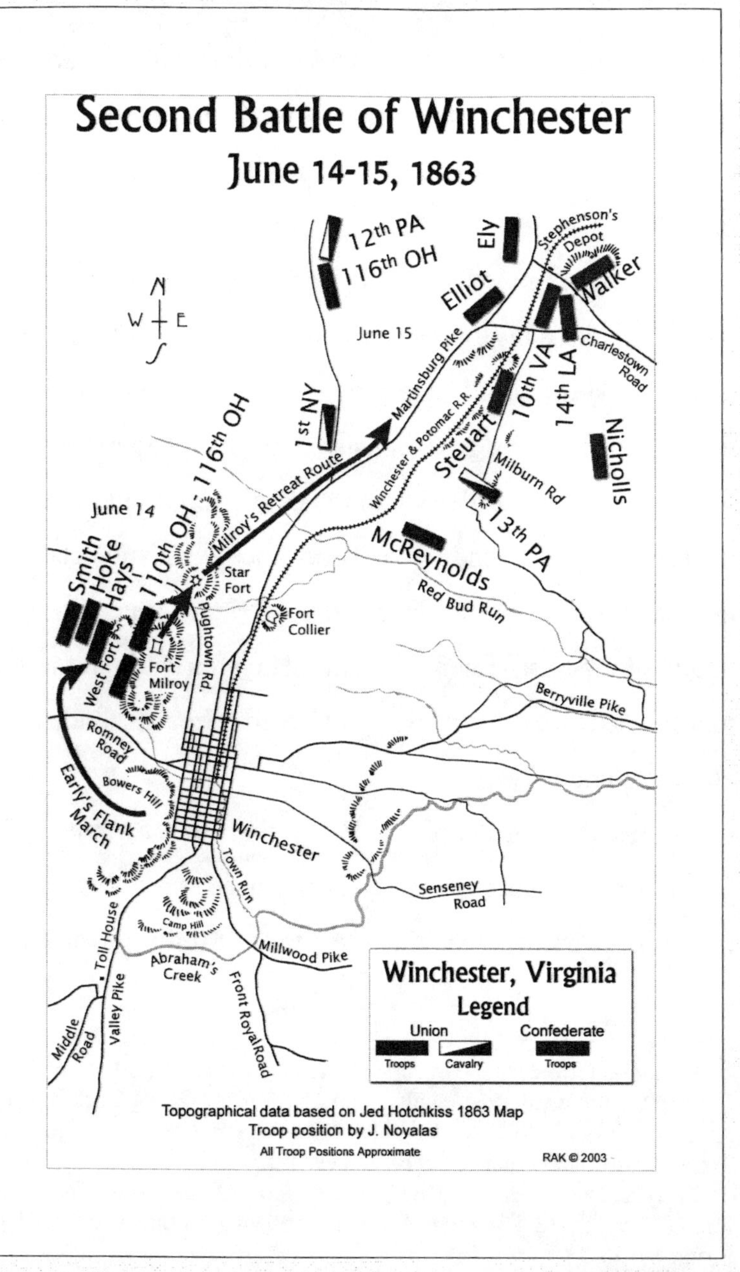

General Early's flank attack on West Fort on June 14, 1863, opened the Second Battle of Winchester. As a result of Early's success, General Milroy decided to withdraw his forces from Winchester late on the night of June 14. Milroy's command headed north toward Harpers Ferry, but General Ewell had sent General Edward Johnnson's division north to cut off Milroy's retreat. In the early morning on June 15, the two sides clashed at Stephenson's Depot, several miles north of Winchester. Johnson crushed the remainder of Milroy's force and captured many of Milroy's command.

passed since this same Louisiana brigade turned the tide of battle at First Winchester. Now they were called to do it again, but this time under a different commander and positioned in a different location. The Federals made a courageous stand but were unable to withstand the sustained Confederate attack. By nightfall, the Union force had withdrawn into Fort Milroy.

As General Ewell's other forces approached Winchester, a lighthearted scene developed. Major Harry Gilmor of the 2nd Maryland Cavalry had a reputation for being a daring, courageous officer and he demonstrated these qualities by challenging Major William Goldsborough of the 2nd Maryland Infantry to a race into the town.[274] As their men cheered and some of the town's women watched, the men dashed for town. Each man later boasted that he had won the race.

As the two Maryland Confederates enjoyed themselves, Milroy's fate hung in the balance. The general from Indiana was not ready to surrender and Kate Sperry – with hope in her heart – added a line to her diary: "Milroy is not ready to surrender yet – so he's firing on our men with his large siege guns – all the Yanks in fortifications."[275]

Around 9 p.m. on June 14, Milroy held a council of war and decided to withdraw from Winchester. Soon, guns were spiked, supplies abandoned, and by 3 a.m. on June 15, his force

---

[274] Driver, 147; Lenora Kohlbus, "Colonel Harry Gilmore, CSA, Maryland Cavalier" *UDC Magazine* (April 2001), 18. Gilmor's name is spelled incorrectly in the title; it does not have an "e."
[275] Sperry, diary entry for June 14, 1863.

was marching toward Harpers Ferry. As the Union garrison withdrew, Mrs. Lee wrote: "…for the first time in six months, the air is not polluted by their immediate presence…"[276]

General Richard Ewell was an 1840 graduate of West Point. During Stonewall Jackson's 1862 Valley Campaign, Ewell contributed immensely to Jackson's success. At Second Winchester, Ewell removed the last major obstacle between the Army of Northern Virginia and the Potomac River. Ewell's action at Winchester was his first major engagement since losing a leg at Groveton in 1862. Ewell remained active in all of the Confederate campaigns through the Battle of Spotsylvania Court House in May 1864. He was injured during the battle by a fall from his horse, and afterwards commanded the Department of Henrico and near the end of the Civil War the defenses of Richmond. He was captured during the Battle of Sayler's Creek on April 6, 1865, and was not released from Fort Warren until August 19, 1865. After this he went to Tennessee where he died in 1872. (Alabama Department of Archives and History)

In the meantime, General Ewell ordered Johnson's division to move north toward Stephenson's Depot, with Lieutenant Colonel R.S. Snowden Andrews' Artillery Battalion in support. As early morning darkness hid the ground at Stephenson's Depot,

---

[276] Lee, diary entry for June 14, 1863.

Johnson's men heard the thud of marching feet. Milroy's column was approaching their position.

Immediately, the two opposing sides clashed and a fight erupted that continued for about an hour into the breaking dawn. Milroy's force was in a state of total confusion and individual units were separated from the main force. Regiments made ill-fated attempts to break the Confederate line, but failed. Confederate General Johnson formed his line of battle facing the Martinsburg Pike, with his center anchored at a bridge across a railroad cut. At the bridge, Lieutenant Colonel Andrews placed two guns to anchor the center of the Confederate line. Numerous Federal assaults were made to take the guns. At the end of the battle the guns remained with only three men to fire them. Old Allegheny's center had held.[277]

Frightened teamsters and sutlers that had scampered out of Winchester added to the confusion in Milroy's column as his Third Brigade, commanded by Colonel Andrew McReynolds, collapsed. Johnson had put the finishing touches on a well-orchestrated plan developed the previous day. Large amounts of supplies were taken and over 3,000 of Milroy's men were captured. Those Union soldiers lucky enough to escape Ewell eventually made it to Harpers Ferry and the units separated from the main Union force made their way to nearby Hancock, Maryland.[278]

---

[277] Beck and Grunder, *The Second Battle of Winchester*, 48.
[278] Henry J. Hunt, "The First Day At Gettysburg" *Battles and Leaders of the Civil War*, 3:265.

With Milroy's defeat, the Valley was clear for an invasion of Pennsylvania. Kate Sperry, hopeful that such an invasion would bring an end to the war in favor of the Confederacy, boasted of Milroy's defeat:

> … we captured, killed, and wounded at least 7,000 and old Milroy hadn't many more – he managed to make his escape, but we got all his stores – sutler's
>
> commissary's [sic], and quartermaster's – it's been a joyful day for us.[279]

While Mrs. Lee was equally overjoyed about Milroy's retreat, she posed a key question in her diary on the night of June 16: "it is glorious for us now; the contrast with our position a week since, is almost painfully happy – can it last?"[280] As she pondered the future, Major Alexander "Sandie" Pendleton, now on General Ewell's staff, requested that some of the town's young women make a Confederate flag to be raised over Fort Jackson, the fortification that was once named Fort Milroy.[281] Two captured Union flags were used to make the Confederate flag that was raised over captured Union soldiers in the fort during a ceremony held on the evening of June 16. Mrs. Lee remained concerned about the longevity of the Confederacy's good fortune, but enjoyed the moment. She described the affair:

---

[279] Sperry, diary entry for June 15, 1863.
[280] Lee, diary entry for June 16, 1863.
[281] Bean, 133.

> Some of the girls have been busy… making a flag for "Fort Jackson"… It was raised this evening at 6 o'clock, but no one intending going from our house, not being willing to take the walk, but unexpectedly, General Ewell sent his carriage, which holds five… I declined going, on the plea of being too old… it was a triumph to raise our flag over the 500 Yankee prisoners in the Fort…[282]

Spirits ran high in Winchester as Lee pressed forward into Pennsylvania.

Meanwhile, General Milroy was placed under arrest by General Halleck on June 27, for the debacle at Winchester.[283] A court of inquiry cleared Milroy of any blame, but he did not get another command until the spring of 1864. He then operated with some success in Tennessee, but nothing erased his debacle at Winchester.

Mrs. Lee soon had an answer to her question "can it last?" as the Army of Northern Virginia suffered a catastrophic defeat at Gettysburg on July 1-3, 1863. Several days after the battle, news of Lee's defeat reached Winchester along with the bodies of the wounded. Once more churches, hotels, warehouses, and private homes were transformed into hospitals for the wounded. Soldiers with more severe wounds remained in Winchester while those who could be transported were moved south to Staunton.[284]

---

[282] Lee, diary entry for June 16, 1863.
[283] Collins, 67.
[284] Quarles, 42.

As the wounded were treated, Union captives were marched through town on July 12. Gettie Miller, the young teenager with a special hatred for anyone in a blue uniform, recorded the scene as she gazed on the stream of blue:

> Yesterday they brought in the yankee prisoners and I think it must have taken them an hour to go through… I don't think our men ought to take them prisoner they ought to shoot everyone [sic] of them…[285]

The Union Army moved south after some indecisiveness following Gettysburg and threatened to cut off Lee's army from Virginia. In order to counter this threat, Confederate forces in Winchester were withdrawn and ordered south. By July 25, the Confederates departed and with them went the hopes of the townspeople. Kate Sperry, with uncertainty and fear wrote: "We will be left at the mercy of the Yanks again."[286] Gettie Miller was disgusted with the withdrawal of Confederate forces and described the depressing scene:

> When we came home we found the town deserted our men had all gone it looks so quiet not to see the soldiers. They have broken up I don't know how many guns and thrown them in the street…[287]

Gettie's mother went down into the littered streets and picked up a ramrod as a memento of the previous military activity.[288]

---

[285] Miller, diary entry for July 13, 1863.
[286] Sperry, diary entry for July 24, 1863.
[287] Miller, diary entry for July 24, 1863.
[288] Ibid., diary entry for July 24, 1863.

On July 26, around 3:30 p.m., Union soldiers reentered Winchester and, according to Kate Sperry, 300 cavalrymen behaved "rather civilly." Aside from tearing up gardens, property damage was kept to a minimum. [289] Captain Charles Coontz's garden fell victim to the troopers as Sperry noted that some of them "tore up Capt. Coontz's garden and rode down [the] street with heads of cabbage sticking on their sabres."[290]

Members of this Union raiding party encountered minor opposition when several dozen Confederates opposed the cavalrymen's entrance into town. The small group of Confederates killed one Union soldier and captured two horses, but was driven out of town.[291] After scouring the area, the Union cavalry withdrew from Winchester around 10 p.m.[292]

More cavalry arrived the following day, but the townspeople were surprised to find it was Major Harry Gilmor with a small contingent of Confederate horsemen. Gilmor remained in town only until July 29, when he was forced to withdraw by Brigadier General William Averell and 500 Union cavalry.[293] Gilmor returned to town on August 7, but left a few hours later when another group of Union cavalry was reported to be bearing down on Winchester.

---

[289] Sperry, diary entry for July 26, 1863.
[290] Ibid.
[291] Ibid.
[292] Ibid.
[293] Delauter, 58.

Thus began an unsettled period with some of the shortest occupations of Winchester during the war. It lasted until the spring of 1864. On August 13, 1863, Lieutenant Colonel Thomas F. Wildes of the 116th Ohio Volunteer Infantry learned of the large amount of government property, including a large quantity of telegraph wire left behind in the town when the Confederate Army left at the end of July.[294] Wildes ordered Major Quinn and 200 men of the 1st New York Cavalry to enter the town, secure government property, and monitor Confederate troop movements in the Valley.[295] The Union raid was a total success and Quinn seized Captain George Shearer, a notorious guerilla, along with four other Rebels, two wagonloads of government property, and some wounded Union soldiers.[296]

The rest of 1863 was filled with uncertainty for Winchester's citizens. Townspeople became hopeful that the town would be kept in Confederate hands when General John D. Imboden's Northwestern Brigade arrived on October 15. Unfortunately, Imboden did not set up a headquarters in the town, and Union soldiers returned on October 20.[297]

As December approached, Union raiders demolished a great deal of property and looted stores in Winchester, but more fighting was still to come for the inhabitants. The evening of New Year's Eve witnessed a small engagement between Union and

---

[294] *O.R.,* Ser. I, Vol. XXIX, Part 1, 74.
[295] Ibid.
[296] Ibid.
[297] Delauter, 60.

Confederate troops in which the Confederates took the upper hand and held the town for the final hours of 1863.[298]

By the end of 1863 many of the town's citizens were refugees. Some hearty souls remained; among them was Mrs. Lee. The feisty woman described how she survived all of the hardship to this point in her diary:

> … I have lost property, have at times been in great danger of life & liberty from our enemies; have endured hardships & privations & have performed manual labor, that in peace times I wish I would have thought impossible – notwithstanding all this, I have gloried, even in my sufferings; not because of the hand that sent them, but from enthusiastic devotion to my beloved country, struggling against tyranny & oppression.[299]

The year closed ominously for Winchester and the entire Confederacy. The South had suffered tremendous losses in 1863. Vicksburg and the Mississippi River were lost, Lee's second attempt at an invasion of the North had failed, and Union forces had pushed Confederate General Braxton Bragg's forces out of southern Tennessee by November, 1863. Control of southern Tennessee provided Union General William T. Sherman with a strategic base for his Atlanta campaign planned for the spring of 1864. Beyond strategic problems, the Confederacy's resources were dwindling even as the Union had not completed its full

---

[298] Ibid., 63.
[299] Lee, diary entry for August 21, 1863.

mobilization. Hope and enthusiastic devotion were the two remaining rallying points for the Confederacy as the Civil War entered its bloodiest year, 1864.

New Year's Day, 1864, found the residents of Winchester in good spirits with hopes high because Confederate troops commanded by Colonel George H. Smith had entered town.[300] This force remained for several days, but it was not intended to have an extended presence. Smith's force was to act as a diversion while Confederate cavalry foraged for supplies in the nearby South Branch Valley.

On January 3, the Union cavalry launched an expedition to Winchester under the command of Colonel William H. Boyd of the 21st Pennsylvania Cavalry.[301] Boyd positioned his unit to cover all entrances except the western approach to the town. Then with 300 men, Boyd charged into town. Six rebels were captured, one was killed, and a Confederate officer identified as Captain Armstrong was wounded in the brief melee.[302] Boyd withdrew as soon as he learned that Major General Fitzhugh Lee's cavalry was expected in Winchester at any moment.[303]

With daily raids throughout the next several months, the townspeople suffered from continued uncertainty about their future. They continued their daily activities as best they could, but

---

[300] Delauter, 63.
[301] *O.R.,* Ser. I, Vol. XXXIII, 11.
[302] Ibid.
[303] Ibid. Fitzhugh Lee was promoted to brigadier general on July 24, 1862 and major general on August 3, 1863.

never knew when or where the next skirmish, battle, or raid would occur.

On the evening of January 14, a worship service at the Market Street Methodist Church was interrupted as four Confederate partisans stormed into the church and arrested William Dooly.[304] According to the Rebels, Dooly was a Union sympathizer and spy.[305]

The accused man's son feared for his father's safety and rode quickly to Union-held Martinsburg where he told the Union commander of his father's capture. Colonel R.S. Rodgers, the Federal commander, sent a message to Mayor William Fuller requesting Dooly's release at once. Rodgers also prepared to send a detachment of Union cavalry to arrest some of Winchester's prominent citizens as a reprisal if Fuller did not promptly comply with the Union officer's order.

Mayor Fuller informed Rodgers that since Dooly was in the service of the United States, he was subject to capture. Colonel Rodgers was not pleased with the mayor's response and carried out his threat. Soon Robert Conrad was arrested; he was once a Unionist leader in the secession convention but he was now a staunch Confederate[306]. Rodgers sent his troops to town again on

---

[304] Delauter, 63.

[305] Douglas Southall Freeman, ed., *Lee's Dispatches*, 162.

[306] According to *Lee's Dispatches*, Conrad was arrested after Reverend Boyd, however the footnote in which this information is found is not clear, the diary entry of Mrs. Lee for this time, January 16, 21, 23, 24, and 28 points to the fact the Conrad was arrested on January 18 and Boyd on January 24.

January 24, to arrest as many prominent Winchester men as possible, but they found and arrested only one man, the Reverend Andrew H.H. Boyd, pastor of the Loudoun Street Presbyterian Church.[307] The stay of the two men in Union captivity was short. Conrad was soon released and Boyd was paroled, but the unfortunate Mr. Dooly's fate is not found in any historical record.

At the end of January, while two of the town's prominent citizens were in captivity, Confederate Brigadier General Thomas Rosser, a dashing cavalier in his late twenties and a close West Point friend of Union officer George Custer, led another Confederate foraging expedition into the troubled area.[308]

The next Union "occupation" did not occur until February 5, and thereafter there was a strong daily Federal presence from February 12-21, caused by the daring attacks of Confederate raider Harry Gilmor. On February 11, for example, Gilmor disabled a section of the Baltimore and Ohio Railroad to hamper Union troop movements from the west.[309] Gilmor succeeded and his success prompted Union forces to move into the vicinity of Winchester to search for the Confederate cavalryman. Over the next ten days, the inhabitants saw constant activity as Union cavalrymen searched for Gilmor, but they failed to find him and ceased searching after February 21.

---

[307] Freeman, ed., *Lee's Dispatches*, 162. Quarles, 121.
[308] Eric J. Wittenberg, *Glory Enough For All: Sheridan's Second Raid And The Battle of Trevilian Station* (Washington D.C.: Brassey's, 2001), 14-15. A description of Rosser appears on these two pages.
[309] Gilmor, 143.

The remainder of February and March saw several brief visits by Union cavalry but there was no major military activity in or near the war worn town. To this point in the war, the town had been subjected to raids, occupations, death, and destruction but nothing had prepared them for the sights they witnessed on April 3. With polished brass buckles, shiny buttons, and new muskets a black regiment marched through the streets of the town. The regiment stayed in Winchester several hours before marching to Martinsburg. Mrs. Lee wrote in her diary:

> I was in my room, & hearing the sound of horses feet looked up & saw a white Yankee officer &, to my inexpressible horror, a company of negro infantry following him; I was near fainting & more unnerved than by any sight I have seen since the war. They were quickly followed by the rest of the black Regt. & are bivouacked in the Market Square, not two hundred yards from us. The creatures are as black as night, & looked cowed & subdued, driven along by their white drivers... there is nothing I have dreaded so much during the war... as being where negro troops were garrisoned.[310]

This was a scene the citizens of Winchester had never anticipated.

The sound of approaching Union cavalry filled the air on April 8, as Major H.W. Hunter led a detachment into town to evict two small companies of Confederate cavalry.[311] Hunter's force consisted of 107 men of the 6th and 7th West Virginia Cavalry and

---

[310] Lee, diary entry for April 3, 1864. No record indicates the regimental designation for this unit.
[311] *O.R.,* Ser. I, Vol. XXXIII, 263-64.

forty-four men from the 14th Pennsylvania Cavalry.[312] The Confederates numbered less than 100 and were feeding and watering their mounts when Hunter's cavalry swept down on them. Caught by surprise, the Rebel cavalrymen quickly mounted and galloped out of town toward safety. Hunter's men pursued the Confederates for one mile and after the brief skirmish Hunter's men returned to town to relax while a detachment of the 14th Pennsylvania acted as a rear guard.[313]

The Confederates regrouped while Hunter's men rested and later in the day entered the town and caught Hunter by surprise. In this confused state Hunter's cavalrymen withdrew in the face of the smaller adversary.[314] Instead of directing his troopers, Hunter was talking with several of Winchester's ladies during the attack and lost control over the incident.[315] His commander, Brigadier General William Averell later placed him under arrest.[316]

May 1864 did not bring spring flowers to Winchester; instead, it brought the first major occupying force since Milroy evacuated the previous year. Significant changes were occurring with the Union Army. President Lincoln had finally found a general who would fight – Lieutenant General Ulysses S. Grant. Grant intended to maneuver all of the Union armies as if they were one. With all Union forces under Grant's command, the

---

[312] Ibid.
[313] Ibid.
[314] Ibid.
[315] Ibid., 265.
[316] Ibid., 263-64.

Shenandoah Valley began to figure as a key part of the Federal Army's grand strategic plan. While Major General William T. Sherman pressed forward in Georgia, General Butler moved toward Richmond and Petersburg, and Major General George Meade's Army of the Potomac moved to attack the Army of Northern Virginia. In the Shenandoah Valley, General Franz Sigel, no stranger to Winchester, moved to cripple the "Breadbasket of the Confederacy" and thereby eliminate Lee's major source of food. Sigel led 7,000 Union troops into Winchester on the first of May.[317] He adhered to strict military discipline and prohibited the townspeople from leaving their home while his men searched every building in the town for contraband. Kate Sperry wrote of Sigel's insensitivity:

> Old Sigel is worse than Milroy, considering the short time he has been here – not a soul has been permitted to leave town or one citizen to come in. Sigel has arrested every boy and man he can find out in the country and a good many of the townspeople.[318]

On May 7, the citizens breathed a sigh of relief as Sigel's Union forces marched south. While Sigel was in Winchester, he and several other officers boarded at Mrs. Hollingsworth's home and on his departure, Sigel paid her five dollars. Sigel's men, however, caused a great deal of damage to her property when they

---

[317] Quarles, 93. The note is in regard to the date that Sigel arrived in Winchester.
[318] Sperry, diary entry for May 7, 1864.

took the flooring out of her mill for a variety of uses. Kate Sperry, although delighted to see the small German general gone, was disgusted at the treatment accorded to Mrs. Hollingsworth.

> Sigel and five of his staff boarded with Mrs. Hollingsworth, and at the end of the week when they were about leaving Sigel gave her $5 as pay besides taking the flooring of their mill, had camp stools and tables made from the lumber and sold them to their own soldiers. What conduct for a General![319]

Sigel marched his command south to New Market and on May 15, clashed with Confederate forces under command of Major General John C. Breckinridge. During the battle, Breckinridge's ranks were being depleted so he turned to his reserve unit – cadets from the Virginia Military Institute – for reinforcements. With great reluctance, Breckinridge turned to Major Charles Semple of his staff and gave the order to put the boys into the battle.[320] The cadets had been activated in seven prior battles but were never engaged in combat. The cadets performed well and helped to seal the Confederate victory at New Market. As a result of the defeat, Sigel was replaced by Major General David Hunter. Two days after the battle, hellish scenes reappeared in Winchester as wagons

---

[319] Sperry, diary entry for May 15, 1864.
[320] William C. Davis, *Breckinridge: Statesman, Soldier, Symbol* (Baton Rouge: Louisiana State University Press, 1974), 425-26.

stacked with bloated Union corpses and the wounded rolled into the town.[321]

After General Hunter replaced the defeated Sigel on May 21, he implemented plans for a new offensive in the Shenandoah Valley. Along with Hunter came the beginning of a scorched earth policy designed to cripple the Confederacy's main agricultural center. After the coming Battle of Piedmont, Hunter marched forward unopposed and left a charred trail through the Valley.

At the Battle of Piedmont on June 5, 1864, Hunter was attacked by a combined force of Confederate infantry and cavalry commanded by Brigadier General William "Grumble" Jones. Jones was killed instantly by a bullet that struck his forehead and the Confederates were defeated. Hunter's victory at Piedmont cleared the Shenandoah Valley of Confederate defenders and allowed him easy passage. Hunter burned the Virginia Military Institute at Lexington and moved to Lynchburg, but on June 18, Hunter withdrew from his position in front of Lynchburg and retreated into the wilderness regions of West Virginia.

Credit for Hunter's withdrawal from the Valley belongs to Brigadier General John McCausland. McCausland's Confederate cavalry slowed Hunter's movements in mid-June to a near halt. With supplies running low and news of the approach of General Jubal A. Early's Second Corps, Army of Northern Virginia, Hunter

---

[321] For a complete study of the Battle of New Market refer to: William C. Davis, *The Battle of New Market* (Baton Rouge: Louisiana State University Press, 1975).

decided to withdraw from Lynchburg. Early was surprised to find no Federals in Lynchburg.[322]

Early was sent to the Valley in mid-June not only to contend with Hunter but to create a strategic diversion. General Grant was pressing Lee hard in the spring 1864 campaigns and, while morale remained high in the Confederate ranks, Lee needed to draw Union forces away from his lines at Petersburg, Virginia. Recalling Jackson's success in the Valley in 1862, Lee believed that a Confederate corps in the Valley might reap significant strategic gains by moving toward Maryland.

General Early's Second Corps, after suppressing Hunter's threat to Lee's rear on June 17, pressed down the Valley toward Winchester. By July 1, Gilmor's Marylanders arrived in town in advance of Early's main body to prevent the Federals from obtaining intelligence concerning Early's movements and intentions.[323] The following day, Gilmor fended off a small body of Union cavalry as the Second Corps arrived south of Winchester. A feeling of security grew among the town's Confederate sympathizers as Early's force moved in.

Early was relaxed knowing that Hunter was not an immediate threat. If there was any consolation for Hunter it was that he was able to retreat without loss until his troops reached West Virginia where hunger and Confederate guerillas began

---

[322] Edward J. Stackpole, *Sheridan in the Shenandoah* (Harrisburg, Pa.: Stackpole Books, 1992) 31-2.
[323] Gilmor, 184, Delauter, 72.

taking a toll. Out of supplies, Hunter's command arrived in Charleston on June 29, and posed no threat to Early's Corps.[324]

At sunrise on July 3, rolling drums and officers voices filled the air, announcing that Early's army was moving. On July 6, Early crossed the Potomac River into Maryland and three days later defeated General Lew Wallace at the Battle of Monocacy. This was the third major Confederate incursion of the war into Maryland.

While Union forces were defeated at the Battle of Monocacy, the action saved Washington D.C. General Wallace, noted in postwar years as the author of *Ben Hur,* was commander of the Union's Middle Department headquartered in Baltimore. Wallace received reports of Early's invasion and set up a line of defense behind the Monocacy River, east of Frederick, Maryland. Early's corps was able to drive Wallace from his position, but his delaying action possibly saved the Union capital. Alarm bells sounded in Washington as the battle at Monocacy raged. Union troops were deployed to the capital's fortifications from Grant's army at Petersburg. When Early reached the outskirts of Washington on July 11, he found that the Union VI Corps had arrived that same morning and had manned the city's defenses. Early, not wanting to jeopardize his corps, withdrew toward Winchester and on June 16, Early's lead elements entered the town.

---

[324] Stackpole, 44. The information for the entire paragraph comes from this page.

In 1862, Wallace was criticized by Grant for failing to aggressively attack the Confederate right flank at the Battle of Shiloh, but his delaying action at Monocacy redeemed Wallace in Grant's eyes. This was 1864 – an election year – and even the temporary loss of Washington, D.C., to Early would probably have spelled defeat at the polls for Lincoln and possibly a victory for the peace candidate, George McClellan, and probably a negotiated end to the war.

After victory at Monocacy, Early stayed briefly in Winchester but pulled out of town during the night of July 19. Early ordered Major General Stephen D. Ramseur, an 1860 graduate of West Point with his first a division command, to march from Berryville, seventeen miles west to Winchester, to block a possible Union advance from Martinsburg.[325]

Ramseur probed north of town throughout the afternoon on July 20. Around 4 p.m. the familiar rattle of musketry began to fill the air. The ensuing engagement at Rutherford's Farm quickly turned sour for Ramseur when he ordered an assault into a strongly fortified Union position. His first attempt at division command was a dismal failure because his force was grossly outnumbered in the engagement by General William Averell's command. Because of the defeat, Ramseur received a great deal of criticism from his men and the Southern press.

---

[325] Gary W. Gallagher, *Stephen Dodson Ramseur: Lee's Gallant General* (Chapel Hill: The University of North Carolina Press, 1995), 131.

Ramseur fell back through Winchester and joined the rest of Early's corps at Fisher's Hill, near Strasburg. Following Averell's rout of Ramseur, Major General Horatio Wright, unjustly confident of the current strength of the Union position in the Valley, ordered the VI and XIX Corps to rejoin the Army of the Potomac near Petersburg where Grant was attempting to hammer Lee into submission.[326] This left the VIII Corps, under Brigadier General George Crook, to contend with the pugnacious Early. "Uncle George," as Crook was sometimes called by his men, bore the brunt of Wright's error in judgment several days later at Kernstown.[327]

Averell's cavalry entered Winchester the day after the victory at Rutherford's Farm and Crook's VIII Corps arrived on July 22. Crook's main force remained slightly north of Winchester, while several regiments of Union cavalry were deployed south of Winchester at Kernstown. On July 23, Confederate cavalry attacked Union cavalry pickets. Crook, believing Early to be no immediate threat, ordered General Alfred Duffie's First Cavalry Division to push the enemy horsemen back.[328] Duffie drove off his opponents with ease.

By noon on July 24, Crook realized that Early was a serious threat and that Wright's decision to send two corps out of the

---

[326] Brandon H. Beck & Roger U. Delauter, *Early's Valley Campaign: The Third Battle of Winchester* (Lynchburg: H.E. Howard, 1997), 4.

[327] Faust, ed., 193.

[328] Martin F. Schmidt, ed., *General George Crook: His Autobiography* (Norman: University of Oklahoma Press, 1946), 123.

region was a serious mistake. On the same day, Early's army appeared in his front at Kernstown. General Breckinridge began the rout of Union forces with an attack against the Union left flank. Major General John B. Gordon, a man unequaled in courage under fire, advanced on Crook's center. To finish off Crook's battered command, Ramseur moved against the Union right and rolled up that portion of Crook's line and redeemed himself for the defeat he suffered at Rutherford's Farm. Crook's corps fled through town in a perfect blue stampede as Rebel cavalry closed on them from behind. Early's cavalry pursued Crook only a few miles north of Winchester and allowed the Union Army to slip away to safety at Harpers Ferry.

Throughout the 1864 Valley Campaign, Early's most serious handicap was the weakness of his cavalry, which proved unsound time and again.[329] Early's cavalry lacked aggressiveness; it also had supply problems to solve and was poorly equipped in comparison with their Union counterpart.[330] By 1864, Union cavalry were armed with state of the art breech loading carbines; some companies were armed with the seven round Spencer carbine. The Confederate horsemen, however, were armed with a

---

[329] A prime example of the ineptness of Early's cavalry came at the Battle of Fisher's Hill, September 22, 1864, where the cavalry under Lunsford Lomax was ordered to protect the Confederate left flank, however seing the Union advance the Confederate cavalry withdrew and left Ramseur's flank exposed.

[330] For more on the problems of Early's cavalry in the Shenandoah Valley in 1864 see Robert K. Krick, "'The Cause of All My Disasters': Jubal A. Early and the Undisciplined Valley Cavalry" in Gary W. Gallagher, ed., *Struggle for the Shenandoah: Essays on the 1864 Valley Campaign* (Kent: Kent State University Press, 1991).

variety of firearms that included muskets. In early September 1864, the cavalrymen in the three brigades under command of Confederate Major General Lunsford Lomax were armed with Enfield rifles. Harry Gilmor in his memoir wrote: "Lomax had three brigades… armed principally with Enfield rifles, and these useless things for mounted men had nearly ruined the whole command. I would rather command a regiment armed with oaken clubs."[331]

While jubilant at the defeat of the Federals at Kernstown, Winchester's staunchly Confederate citizens saw no point in needlessly punishing prisoners of war. Mrs. Lee was second to none in support for the Confederate cause, but she was sickened by reports of the mistreatment of Union soldiers captured at Kernstown, writing that:

> … the Yankees prisoners have had nothing to eat
> for several days; it made me miserable to think of
> the creatures being starved. Found there was some
> truth in the rumor, but today they had rations
> and tomorrow will have full ones.[332]

As Early's victorious troops moved north through town, Confederate cavalry under the twenty-seven year old General John McCausland burned Chambersburg, Pennsylvania, on July 30. Early ordered the raid to collect ransom to compensate for the damage done by Union General Hunter in the Lower Valley. During his Washington Campaign, which culminated in victory at

---

[331] Gilmor, 245.
[332] Lee, diary entry for July 27, 1864.

Monocacy, Early collected $200,000 ransom in Frederick, Maryland, and $20,000 in Hagerstown, Maryland.[333] Mrs. Lee had witnessed so much destruction in the Valley and felt no sympathy for the inhabitants of Chambersburg. "I cordially approve of the act as a military necessity forced on us by three year's [sic] outrages," she wrote.[334]

Infuriated by Crook's loss at Kernstown, Grant cancelled the VI Corps' movement to Petersburg, ordered the XIX Corps to stay in the region, and reorganized the Valley command. Thirty-three year old cavalry corps commander Major General Philip H. Sheridan was Grant's and Lincoln's choice as the new commander of the new Middle Military Division. Sheridan was an 1853 graduate of West Point and had distinguished himself in earlier battles in the West and Grant gained interest in Sheridan after the latter's men charged up Missionary Ridge during the Battle of Chattanooga. Secretary of War Stanton and General Halleck thought that Sheridan was too young and inexperienced for the position, but Grant assured everyone that Sheridan was the man for the job.[335]

The new Middle Military Division combined the Department of the Susquehanna, the Middle Department, the

---

[333] Millard K. Bushong, *Old Jube: A Biography of General Jubal A. Early* (Shippensburg, Pa.: White Mane Publishing, 1990), 222.
[334] Lee., diary entry for August 3, 1864.
[335] For more on the political struggle that was going on over choosing a commander for the Middle Military Division refer to Gallagher, ed., *Struggle for the Shenandoah*, 41-3.

Department of Washington, and the Department of the West. Sheridan took command on August 6, 1864, and had under his command his old West Point roommate, General Crook.

After winning at Kernstown, Early probed north of Winchester, but stayed in the vicinity and Confederate soldiers again were a common sight in town. Soon, rumors spread that Early was going to withdraw, and on August 10, he moved south.[336] Hattie Griffith's sentiment seemed to tilt toward the Union as she wrote on August 12: "The Rebel army under Early left us yesterday. Some Federal Cavalry came in and we felt once more in the U.S."[337]

For three days after Early's departure, Federal soldiers occupied Winchester and Brigadier General John R. Kenly commanded the garrison. A delighted Hattie Griffith wrote: "General Kenly had command of the town about two days – troops moving and a very great excitement. Some of the 19th Corps and the Zouaves have Provost duty to do."[338]

Sheridan set about organizing his 40,000 troops to deal with Early, but General Lee, troubled by the Union buildup, sent reinforcements to Early. Major General Joseph Kershaw's infantry division, Major Wilfred Cutshaw's artillery battalion, and Major General Fitzhugh Lee's cavalry division moved west across the

---

[336] Delauter, 75.
[337] Griffith, diary entry for August 12, 1864.
[338] Ibid., diary entry for August 13, 1864.

Blue Ridge to reinforce the battered Second Corps.[339] On August 12, Grant learned of Lee's plan to reinforce the small Confederate force in the Shenandoah Valley and quickly ordered Sheridan not to engage Early until he could ascertain the position of all elements of Early's command.[340]

Sheridan pulled back from positions near Strasburg to locations closer to Harpers Ferry on the night of August 15. He posted Brigadier General Alfred Torbert's cavalry on the Valley Pike to prevent a major engagement, but on August 17, Torbert was attacked by Confederate horsemen and infantry that pushed him back through Winchester.[341] Hattie Griffith described the perilous scene:

> Just at dusk the musketry was so rapid and so much of it. Then the wagons came and then a brisk retreat through, the Federals came back and drew up in line… They fought through the town, a great many bullets striking our house… It was the sixth battle we have had here and the third in town this summer. Soon after eight o'clock, the Rebels were in town and oh, such a time.[342]

Sheridan set up a strong defensive line near Halltown that kept him close to his logistical base at Harpers Ferry. For the next month Early moved stealthily and held Sheridan at bay while the men of the Second Corps were involved in skirmishes and

---

[339] Beck and Delauter, *The Third Battle of Winchester*, 15.
[340] U.S. Grant, *Personal Memoirs of U.S. Grant* (New York: Charles L. Webster & Co., 1886), 2:327.
[341] Delauter, 76.
[342] Griffith, diary entry for August 17, 1864.

plundering. An outraged Hattie Griffith attested to the conduct of Early's men writing: "The Rebs have taken all our bees and vegetables…"[343] While Hattie groaned about the loss, Confederate spirits in town ran high because Early remained nearby.

Even with a far superior force numerically, "Little Phil" Sheridan did not want to attack Early without knowing, for certain, Early's strength and position. Sheridan needed an informant behind Confederate lines to obtain intelligence on Early's strength, plans, and intentions. Sheridan soon learned that a slave, Thomas Laws of nearby Millwood, possessed a Confederate permit to move in and out of Winchester three times a week to sell vegetables to the townspeople.[344] After convincing Laws to serve as a courier, Sheridan needed to find a Union loyalist in Winchester who was willing to gather information about Early's army.

Sheridan discussed the matter with his subordinate, General Crook. Crook told Sheridan he knew of someone who might help, a woman named Rebecca Wright. Wright had first caught Crook's attention in July before the Union defeat at Kernstown. Crook frequented Wright's home for dinner and was impressed by her loyalty to the Union.[345]

---

[343] Ibid., diary entry for August 21, 1864.

[344] Phillip H. Sheridan, *The Personal Memoirs of P.H. Sheridan* (New York: DaCapo Press, 1992), 276. Beck and Delauter, *The Third Battle of Winchester*, 23.

[345] Sylvia G.L. Dannett, "Rebecca Wright – Traitor or Patriot?" *Lincoln Herald* (Fall 1963), 104.

Wright was a young Quaker schoolteacher in town and was the only hope Sheridan had of gaining intelligence from behind Rebel lines. Sheridan wrote a short message to Rebecca Wright on tissue paper. He wadded the message into a small pellet, wrapped it in tin foil, and instructed Thomas Laws to carry it inside his mouth and swallow the note if he was halted and questioned by Confederate guards.[346] Laws made it safely to Wright's home and gave her the message. While initially hesitant, Rebecca Wright decided that when Laws returned the following day for Sheridan's answer she would risk her life to help the Union. The note from Sheridan read:

> I learn from Major – General Crook that you are a loyal lady, and still love the old flag. Can you inform me of the position of Early's forces, the number of divisions in his army, and the strength of any or all of them, and his probably or reported intentions? Have any more troops arrived from Richmond, or are any more coming, or reported to be coming?
> I am, very respectfully, your most obedient servant,
> P.H. Sheridan, Major – General Commanding.
> You can trust the bearer.[347]

On the night of September 14, Wright's mother was visited by a Confederate soldier who told her that Kershaw's division and Cutshaw's artillery had left Winchester to rejoin Lee. Rebecca Wright relayed this message to Sheridan on September 16, and

---

[346] Sheridan, 276
[347] Ibid., 277-78.

"Little Phil" set in motion a plan to strike Early.[348]   Wright's message to Sheridan read:

> I have no communication whatever with the rebels, but will tell you what I know. The division of General Kershaw, and Cutshaw's artillery, twelve guns and men, General Anderson commanding, have been sent away, and no more are expected, as they cannot be spared from Richmond. I do not know how the troops are situated, but the force is much smaller than represented. I will take pleasure hereafter in learning all I can of their strength and position, and the bearer may call again.
> Very respectfully yours[349]

This intelligence could not have come at a better time for General Sheridan, for Grant wanted action but for the past month he had not engaged Early. As a result of this inactivity, General Grant went to the Valley to meet with Sheridan. On September 15, Grant arrived in Charles Town and summoned Sheridan to meet with him. Sheridan met with Grant in Charles Town shortly after Wright sent Sheridan the news of Kershaw's and Cutshaw's withdrawal. When Sheridan informed Grant of the intelligence he received and of his plan to attack Winchester, Grant kept a plan he had devised to himself and simply ordered "Little Phil" to "Go in!"[350]

---

[348] Sheridan, 278.
[349] Ibid.
[350] Grant, 2:326-27.

Rebecca Wright, a young teacher and a Quaker, was one of Winchester's staunch Union supporters. The information that she supplied Sheridan on September 16, 1864, gave him the added confidence to attack Early at Winchester on September 19, 1864. (Handley Regional Library)

Early committed a serious error on September 17. He divided his force by sending the divisions of John B. Gordon and Major General Robert Rodes to attack Martinsburg and the Baltimore and Ohio Railroad, General John C. Breckinridge's division to Bunker Hill, and left only Ramseur's division to defend Winchester.[351]

As Kershaw and Cutshaw moved to Petersburg, Sheridan stood poised to attack Early at Winchester. The stage was now set for the last and bloodiest of the Winchester battles.

---

[351] Beck and Delauter, *The Third Battle of Winchester*, 20.

Sheridan's sleepy men were roused at 2 a.m. on a rainy and cold Monday morning, September 19, put in formation and marched westward.[352] Simultaneously, Union Brigadier General James H. Wilson, an overly ambitious cavalry officer, led his 3,300 troopers to Winchester on the Berryville Pike as the van of Sheridan's main body.[353] Wilson's task was clearing the Berryville Pike so the VI and XIX Corps had easy passage through the narrow defile known locally as the Berryville Canyon. Once through, the two corps were ordered to attack Ramseur's Confederates in Winchester.

Wilson secured the path for Sheridan's army when he crossed the Opequon Creek at Spout Spring at daybreak. The first shots of the battle sounded in the breaking dawn as men of the 23rd North Carolina fired at Wilson's approaching troopers.[354]

A North Carolina lawyer turned soldier, Brigadier General Robert Johnston, commanded one of Ramseur's brigades and was first to encounter the Federals. Ramseur's force totaled slightly

---

[352] Lewis G. Schmidt, *A Civil War History of the 47th Regiment of Pennsylvania Veteran Volunteers* (Allentown, Pa.: Self published, 1986), 625, in reference to the weather conditions.

[353] Jeffry D. Wert, *From Winchester to Cedar Creek: The Shenandoah Campaign of 1864* (Mechanicsburg, Pa.: Stackpole Books, 1997), 47.

[354] Wesley Merrit, "Sheridan in the Shenandoah Valley" *Battles and Leaders of the Civil War*, 4:507; Beck and Delauter, *The Third Battle of Winchester*, 28.

more than 2,000 and these troops contended with the weight of two Union corps until reinforcements arrived.

As Wilson's troopers and Ramseur's infantry battled, Brigadier General Wesley Merritt's division of Union cavalry attempted to cross over two fords on the Opequon several miles

Major General Philip H. Sheridan was viewed by many officials in Washington as being too young for the command of the newly created Middle Military Division. Sheridan, an 1853 graduate of West Point, gained recognition from General Grant after his troops charged up Missionary Ridge during the Battle of Chattanooga. Sheridan's 1864 Valley Campaign lasted exactly one month. It began with a victory at Winchester on September 19, 1864, and culminated in victory on October 19, 1864, at the Battle of Cedar Creek. In March 1865 Sheridan went east to be with General Grant for the final month of the war. After the Civil War Sheridan remained in the military and continued to serve until his death in 1888. (Author's Collection)

north of Winchester. Brigadier General George A. Custer's cavalry brigade, of Merrit's division, made several attempts to secure Locke's Ford and finally did so around 9 a.m.[355] While Custer was occupied at Locke's Ford, the rest of Merritt's division crossed the Opequon to the south at Seiver's Ford.

Once the Berryville Pike was secured, Sheridan ordered Major General Horatio Wright's VI Corps to move toward Winchester with all possible haste. Wright, however, showed no speed and placed the VI Corps' wagons and caissons behind his column thereby slowing down the trailing XIX Corps. The resulting traffic jam delayed Sheridan's assault for several hours. This sluggish pace also allowed Early to get Gordon's and Rodes' divisions into defensive positions to meet the two Union corps.[356] Sheridan's line was at last ready to advance at 11:30 a.m.[357]

When the two Union corps were aligned to advance, a shot rang out at 11:40 a.m. to mark the beginning of the Union assault. In response, sulphurous smoke filled the air as Early's cannons roared and hurled iron shells into the Union attackers. Sheridan's troops pressed forward to the Rebel line where they were greeted with a salvo of canister. As the assault fully developed, a wide gap opened in Sheridan's line and Early seized the opportunity to counterattack. Rodes' division surged forward in a perfect wave at this moment; Brigadier General Cullen Andrews Battle's brigade,

---

[355] Beck and Delauter, *The Third Battle of Winchester*, 33.
[356] Stackpole, 203.
[357] Merritt, 4:507.

with the 3rd Alabama Infantry in the lead pressed the Union attackers.[358]

As the counterattack commenced, an artillery fragment struck Rodes and wounded him mortally. General Battle, as the division's senior brigadier, assumed command after Rodes fell. Mistakenly, however, General Early sent orders to General Bryan Grimes, another of Rodes' brigadiers, to take command of the division. Just at the moment the Union line was breaking under Confederate pressure, Grimes rode up and down the lines and ordered a halt to the counterattack. On seeing this, General Battle sent Major Henry Shorter to find Early and clear up the command confusion. Early quickly realized his error and put Battle back in command, but the Confederates had lost their opportunity.[359] This error cost the Confederates dearly as the confusion allowed Union Brigadier General David Russell to advance his division thereby terminating any hope of a successful Rebel counterassault.[360]

As the Union attack stalled on the plateau east of town, Early ordered General Breckinridge to move General Gabriel Wharton's division closer to town. The order reached Breckinridge around 12:30 p.m.[361]

---

[358] Brandon H. Beck, ed., *Third Alabama! The Civil War Memoir of Brigadier General Cullen Andrews Battle, CSA* (Tuscaloosa: University of Alabama Press, 2000), 126; Merritt, 509.
[359] Beck, *Third Alabama!* 126.
[360] Merritt, 4:509.
[361] *O.R.*, Ser. I, Vol. 43, Part 2, 875.

Around the same time Early prepared this dispatch, Sheridan ordered the VIII Corps, until then held in reserve, to move forward. Early lacked any reserves and Sheridan intended to use his manpower advantage to crush the Confederates as Crook's VIII Corps marched closer to town from the east.

At the mouth of the Berryville Canyon, Sheridan and Crook discussed the possibilities of their situation. The right side of Early's line remained strong and Sheridan ordered Crook to strike Early's left flank with his fresh troops. This was the first of two blows Sheridan aimed against Early's left flank. Sheridan ordered Crook to march north, cross Red Bud Run, and then move east along the small creek's northern bank before crossing south again near Hackwood to assault the left side of Early's line.

With the exception of Colonel George S. Patton's brigade, the remainder of Wharton's division contested Crook's advance. Confederate artillery poured devastating fire into Crook's men as they crossed Red Bud Run and deployed into the fields around Hackwood. After the VIII Corps crossed and formed its line of battle around 2 p.m. near Hackwood, it attacked in an attempt to turn Early's left.[362]

As the battle raged, Wharton bolstered his line by placing Chapman's Battery, supported by the 22nd Virginia Infantry, in

---

[362] Richard R. Duncan, ed., *Alexander Neil and the Last Shenandoah Valley Campaign: Letters of an Army Surgeon to his Family, 1864* (Shippensburg: White Mane, 1996), 67. Note: Hackwood refers to the name of a home built in 1777 along Red Bud Run

Fort Collier.[363] The remainder of Patton's brigade, the 23rd and 26th Virginia Infantry Battalions filed in on the left of the 22nd Virginia. Much of Patton's force and the artillery inside Fort Collier were comprised of men from West Virginia. Oddly enough, several of the Union regiments that would later confront the Confederates at Winchester were also from West Virginia.[364]

By late afternoon, the battle was undecided. The Confederate line began to be drawn inward, taking the shape of an inverted "L." By 4:30 p.m. Early's left had been contained by Crook's men and was now anchored several hundred yards north of town at Fort Collier. When young Harriet Griffith visited the fort during its construction in 1861 she expressed a wish in her diary: "… I hope it will never be used."[365] Her hope was about to be shattered as an attack force composed of 6,000 experienced Union cavalrymen prepared for a second and final blow against Early's left flank.

Several miles north of town at Stephenson's Depot, 6,000 Union cavalrymen readied themselves. First at a walk, then a trot, a canter, and finally at a gallop these Federal horsemen, with their sabers glistening in the sun, charged headlong into the Confederate left flank. Colonel William H. Powell's and Colonel James Schoonmaker's cavalry brigades moved west of the Martinsburg Pike; Brigadier General George Custer's brigade moved on the

---

[363] J.L. Scott, *Lowry's, Bryan's, and Chapman's Batteries of Virginia Artillery* (Lynchburg: H.E. Howard, 1988), 91.
[364] Wert, 312. A survey of the order of battle and troop positions reveals this.
[365] Griffith, diary entry for August 21, 1861.

Martinsburg Pike; and Brevet Brigadier General Thomas Devin's and Colonel Charles Lowell's cavalry brigades charged east of the pike.[366]

The VI and XIX Corps had pressed Early's line that faced east, and now the cavalry attack, followed by Crook's VIII Corps, pressed that part of the Confederate line facing north. This powerful cavalry stroke was too much for the battle weary Confederates. Patton's brigade, beginning first with the western Virginians of the 22nd Virginia, collapsed under the shock of the cavalry blows and Early's other units soon followed suit.[367] Early still hoped to salvage some part of the battle and ordered Brigadier General Bryan Grimes to pull back his left flank and turn to engage the threat from the north. Grimes' men fought all day against the VI and XIX Corps but as his men faced north they saw only utter chaos in the Confederate formations. Grimes watched many soldiers fleeing, and detected the fear and a desire to flee in his command. He ordered his men to hold their ground and even threatened to shoot them if they broke for the rear.[368]

Regardless of Early's orders, Grimes' force was no match for the numbers of soldiers deployed by Sheridan. It was this

---

[366] Beck and Delauter, *The Third Battle of Winchester*, 64.

[367] Terry D. Lowry, *22nd Virginia Infantry* (Lynchburg, Va.: H.E. Howard, 1988), 74.

[368] T. Harrell Allen, *Lee's Last Major General: Bryan Grimes of North Carolina* (Mason City, Ia.: Savas Publishing, 1999), 189.

manpower advantage that contributed largely to Early's defeat at Third Winchester and in the Shenandoah Valley in 1864.[369]

In the melee that followed the Union attack, Early's army fell into a state of complete confusion. Colonel Patton rose in his stirrups as he attempted to rally his decimated brigade in a narrow Winchester street when he was struck in the right hip by a shell fragment.[370] As Confederate soldiers stampeded south through town, Patton lay mortally wounded. Patton was captured and taken to the home of Philip Williams on Piccadilly Street where he died on September 25.[371] Frightened citizens pleaded with the scattered Confederate soldiers to turn around and fight. The pleas fell on deaf ears as the men retreated south.

General Ramseur reorganized his division, which had fought the longest that day, reforming it in a defensive position on a ridge that ran through the Mount Hebron Cemetery.[372] Here Ramseur, along with Bryan Grimes' brigade, delayed the pursuing

---

[369] William B. Feis, "Neutralizing The Valley: The Role of Military Intelligence In The Defeat of Jubal Early's Army Of The Valley, 1864 – 1865" *Civil War History* (September 1993), 199. The article details various reasons for Early's defeat in the Valley, Sheridan's numerical superiority being one of them.

[370] Lowry, 74.

[371] Robert H. Patton, *The Pattons: A Personal History of an American Family* (Washington D.C.: Brassey's 1994), 58; Delauter, 80; *O.R.,* Ser. I, Vol. 43, part 1, 597. The Assistant Inspector General of the Brigade, Wood Bouldin, Jr., submitted the following report: "In the hard – fought battle of Winchester, on the 19th, the brigade organization was almost broken up. Col. George S. Patton, commanding the brigade, an officer of highest gallantry and standing and a gentleman irreproachable in character, was left in the hands of the enemy mortally wounded."

[372] Beck and Delauter, *The Third Battle of Winchester*, 68.

Third Battle of Winchester
September 19, 1864

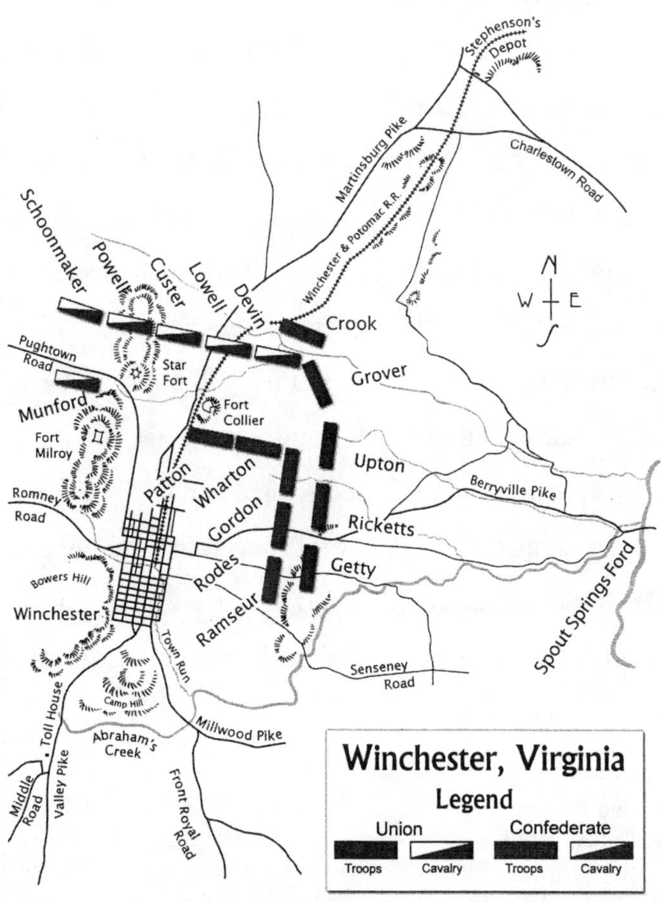

Topographical data based on Jed Hotchkiss 1863 Map
Troop position by J. Noyalas
All Troop Positions Approximate

RAK © 2003

This map details the final phase of the Third Battle of Winchester, the cavalry attack on the Confederate left flank at Fort Collier. The battle began with the Union XIX and VI Corps attacking the Confederate line facing east. After the forces here were contained and pushed back to Winchester, Sheridan ordered a cavalry attack against the Confederate left. Early's battered command retreated through Winchester, south to Fisher's Hill

Yankees long enough for Early's army to get on the Valley Pike and retreat south.

General Jubal A. Early graduated from West Point in 1837. Initially, Early was opposed to secession, however, he decided to defend his native state of Virginia. At the beginning of the war Early commanded the 24th Virginia Infantry and performed admirably during the campaigns in the east, including the Second Battle of Winchester. "Old Jube" arrived in the Shenandoah Valley in the beginning of June 1864. He was successful in clearing it of Federals and came within eyeshot of the United States Capitol Dome in Washington D.C. Throughout the summer of 1864 Early controlled the Valley. However, with his stunning victory at the Second Battle of Kernstown (July 24, 1864) came dramatic changes in Union strategy. Early, greatly outnumbered in the Valley, since September 1864 fought ably, but was crushed by the superior manpower of Sheridan's army. After the Civil War he returned to Lynchburg and continued his law practice. He became the first president of the Southern Historical Society. Early died in 1894. (*Battles and Leaders of the Civil War*)

That evening the sun set on both Winchester and Early's army. Hopes of Winchester's civilians also collapsed as the Federals began another occupation. While Early's cavalrymen were ineffective in the Valley, they were not entirely responsible for this loss. Kate Sperry did, however, blame the cavalry as she wrote: "Had a terrible battle at Winchester yesterday – our Army had to fall back on account of the Cavalry running. They ought to put the Cav[alry] in the Army – every disaster is caused by the Cavalry."[373]

The gruesome aftermath of battle appeared once more. This was the largest and bloodiest of the Winchester battles, and more dead and wounded lay on the fields of Winchester than ever before.[374] Signs were not needed to mark the buildings used as hospitals. Instead, large piles of amputated limbs outside of windows and doors served as locators. Mrs. Lee reported: "They have taken for their hospitals the Taylor Hotel, N. Methodist, German Reformed, Dr. Boyd's [Loudoun Street Church] and Lutheran Churches and Mr. Logan's House..."[375]

Citizens worried about their loved ones that might have perished or lay wounded on the field, but they were not allowed to tend to these unfortunate souls. "They have not brought in ... all of theirs and they will not allow any citizens to go to the field lest

---

[373] Sperry, diary entry for September 20, 1864.

[374] During the First Battle of Winchester the Confederates suffered 400 casualties and the Federals suffered 2,019. The Confederates at Second Winchester suffered 269 casualties, while the Federals under Milroy's command suffered 3,801. At Third Winchester, Early's army suffered 3,500 casualties and General Sheridan's army suffered 5,018. First and Second Winchester combined (6,489) did not produce the losses incurred at Third Winchester (8,518). The casualty figures were taken from Northern Virginia Daily, *Standing Ground: The Civil War in the Shenandoah Valley* (Strasburg, Va.: Shenandoah Publishing House, 1996), 189, 192, 196.

[375] Lee, diary entry for September 20, 1864.

we should count their unburied dead..." noted an aggravated Mrs. Lee.[376]

Spring Mill along the Opequon Creek served as a hospital for the Union VI Corps during the Third Battle of Winchester. (*Battles and Leaders of the Civil War*)

Sheridan's medical director, James T. Ghiselin, confronted problems of his own as there were not enough buildings to handle the wounded soldiers. With all available buildings in use for wounded Union and Confederate troops, Ghiselin ordered a gigantic tent hospital set up at Shawnee Spring on the southern edge of town.[377] 400 hospital tents along with ample medical

---

[376] Ibid.
[377] Beck and Delauter, *The Third Battle of Winchester*, 75.

supplies were shipped to Winchester from Harpers Ferry.[378] The southeast end of town was transformed into a canvas city under the direction of Surgeon John Brinton.[379]

Upon conclusion of the battle a victorious Sheridan rode into town. His first stop was the home of Rebecca Wright.[380] This is the first time Sheridan ever met this courageous Unionist. Wright's clandestine message regarding Early's strength provided Sheridan with the advantage over the Confederates and an opportunity to seize victory. The Union victory at Third Winchester marked the beginning of the end for the Confederacy in the Shenandoah Valley. Confederate forces never enjoyed another victory there.

Sheridan did not pause to rest. He aggressively pressed Early's command south. To garrison Winchester he detached the Third Brigade, First Division, VI Corps, commanded by Colonel Oliver Edwards. Edwards placed the 37th Massachusetts in town as provost, while the other regiments of his brigade, the 49th, 82nd, and 119th, Pennsylvania Infantry Regiments, the 5th Rhode Island and 5th Wisconsin Infantry Battalions, were placed in locations around the perimeter of the town.[381]

---

[378] Clarence Geier, Warren Hofstra, and Joseph A. Whitehorne, "The Sheridan Military Field Hospital Complex at Shawnee Springs", *Winchester – Frederick County Historical Society Journal* 6, (1993), 20.
[379] Geier, et. al., 20.
[380] Delauter, 81.
[381] Wert, 308; Delauter, 81.

Sheridan pursued Early and defeated him at Fisher's Hill on September 22. He continued south to remove Early's presence in the Valley. On October 9, Union cavalry routed their opposition at Tom's Brook and Sheridan, comfortable with the situation, accepted an invitation from Secretary of War Stanton to visit Washington. Sheridan left the army under the command of General Wright, while he and four staff officers departed the Valley on the evening of October 15.[382]

As news of the Confederate defeats and additional wounded soldiers poured into town the citizens' hopes were dashed; many stopped hoping. The citizens adjusted to another Union occupation as Sheridan's forces now controlled the entire Valley. Union soldiers were better behaved than in their previous occupations and a demoralized Mrs. Lee noted: "… I have not heard of many outrages so far except robbing the gardens and chicken coops."[383]

Sheridan compounded the Confederates' military defeat by burning the Shenandoah Valley's harvest from Harrisonburg to Strasburg. This action undercut the Confederate Army's ability to feed itself and the Third Battle of Winchester and the "Great Burning" left Early with two choices: he could leave the Valley or attempt to drive Sheridan out. Early decided on the latter. In mid-October, Sheridan rested comfortably in Washington, while his

---

[382] Wert., 172.
[383] Lee, diary entry for September 20, 1864.

troops established camps near Middletown along the north bank of Cedar Creek.

Early's army marched north during the night of October 18, through the damp, cold air toward Middletown. Early was ready to risk everything in a final battle with Sheridan's army.

Confederate Generals Gordon and Ramseur met during the night of October 18, 1864, while their commands marched north toward Middletown. During that same night, General Sheridan returned to Winchester from Washington. He was completely unaware of the Confederates' approach.

Concealed in early morning fog on October 19, Confederate Major General Joseph Kershaw's division engaged the unsuspecting Federals of the VIII Corps south of Middletown along Cedar Creek. The Federals soon were pushed back and by 5:30 a.m., Early's other divisions had joined the attack. The battle was only a half hour long by 5:30, when the Union VIII Corps had been forced to withdraw and "Old Jube's" Confederates moved closer to Middletown to confront the Union XIX Corps. Sheridan was still in Winchester when he learned of the battle south of Middletown. Sheridan decided to direct his troops in person and around 9 a.m. mounted his trusty steed Rienzi and rode swiftly to Middletown.[384] Winchester's high-spirited women were soon bidding a fond farewell to Sheridan from their windows and doors

---

[384] Sheridan, 319.

by shaking their skirts at him in an unlady-like manner.[385]

By late morning Early had pushed the surprised Union Army back but Sheridan, around 10:30 a.m., had begun to rally his confused units. As the Union troops began to reorganize, Early halted his attack and believed the battle was won. Around 4 p.m., however, Sheridan ordered a massive counterattack. With cavalry on both flanks, Sheridan's command surged forward to Early's line and quickly crushed Early's ragged force.

A steady stream of wounded poured back into Winchester, extinguishing the flickering hopes of pro-Confederate civilians .

View of the Valley Pike where General Sheridan joined his army on October 19 (*Battles and Leaders of the Civil War*)

---

[385] Ibid., 320.

The news of Early's defeat in the battle of Cedar Creek and the news of General Ramseur's death deepened the town's despair on October 20.

Four days after his October 19, victory at Cedar Creek, Sheridan issued an order calling for the arrest of all civilian males between the ages of eighteen and forty-five who supported the local Confederate partisans.[386] The order was issued to restrict the activities of John Singleton Mosby and John H. McNeill. No longer having to worry about Early, Sheridan focused his attention on Mosby's and McNeill's rangers. As long as the partisans remained in the Valley they could disrupt and delay Sheridan's operations.

John S. Mosby was feared by the Union commanders who operated in northern and western Virginia. He was a bit of a ruffian in his teenage years and was imprisoned for shooting one of his classmates from the University of Virginia. When the Civil War broke out he joined the Confederate cavalry and soon served as a valued scout for General J.E.B. Stuart. After winning an independent partisan command in 1862, he hampered Union movements for the next three years throughout Virginia.

Mosby's peer operating in northern and western Virginia was John H. McNeill. Born in Virginia, he spent most of his early life in Missouri. There he served as captain of a company of militia during the secession crisis and was arrested. After being

---

[386] Delauter, 84.

released from Union captivity in 1861 he fled Missouri for Virginia with his three sons. In the summer of 1862 he was made captain of Company E, 18th Virginia Cavalry, known as McNeill's Rangers. The force most often operated independently and constantly raided railroads, captured supplies, and hampered the movement of Union troops, especially in western Virginia.

Mrs. Lee despised Sheridan for issuing what she considered petty edicts, writing in her diary about his bold order to arrest male citizens: "nearly every man in Winchester, young & old was arrested and taken out of pique..."[387] Mosby's progress was not at all hampered. On October 25, his men captured General Alfred Duffie several miles north of town.[388]

Special Union units were organized to deal with Mosby. One element came from Crook's division and was commanded by Captain Richard Blazer. This group of 100 men was formed as a counter-partisan force in central West Virginia and they carried seven shot Spencer carbines. Unfortunately their advanced weaponry proved of little use. Sheridan attempted to end Mosby's operations, but on November 18, 1864, Mosby's men struck again and defeated a force of sixty-two soldiers and captured Captain Blazer near Kabletown, West Virginia, approximately twenty miles northeast of Winchester.[389] Sheridan continued to attempt to

---

[387] Lee, diary entry for October 25, 1864.
[388] Delauter, 85.
[389] Horace Newborn, "The Operations of Mosby's Rangers", *Blue & Gray*, (Summer 2000), 50.

halt Mosby's operations but he and his subordinates were unable to stop the Confederate partisan.

As the November days passed, Winchester's civilians adjusted to the immediate presence of Union winter camps. Sheridan needed to protect the reopened Winchester and Potomac Railroad from sabotage; the road had just been rebuilt after having been torn apart in the early years of the war.[390]

Early in November, Sheridan moved his camps from Belle Grove in Middletown, closer to Kernstown where he set up headquarters at the home of Joseph Mahaney.[391] Mahaney, a wealthy Irishman and a strong supporter of the Union, had been arrested by Stonewall Jackson in March, 1862, when Jackson withdrew from Winchester.[392] Now his two-story brick home was used by a general more to his liking. Also, with the Union's position secure, officers' wives were permitted to stay with their husbands for the winter. Among the wives was Elizabeth "Libbie" Custer, wife of General George Armstrong Custer. "Libbie" joined her husband in Winchester in early November.[393]

On December 1, Sheridan reported that Early was no longer a threat and he ordered the transfer of some units to the Union position at Petersburg. Although the sight of blue columns departing inspired the townspeople for a moment, the Union Army

---

[390] Duncan, 83.
[391] Delauter, 85.
[392] Ecelbarger, 82-3.
[393] Quarles, 100.

was in Winchester to stay. This was the largest Union force the area had experienced and it placed a heavy burden on already drastically depleted local food and wood supplies. Union soldiers, for example, used any piece of wood they could find for heat and construction of winter huts.

The weather was treacherous as Christmas neared. Streets and camps were nearly impassable, soldiers were often unable to move, and horses were frequently seen stuck in mud half way up their legs.[394] Approximately two weeks before Christmas, Sheridan made final adjustments for the winter as one of his divisions prepared to move to Petersburg. Sheridan now moved his quarters to the Logan residence. By December 14, the army was ready to move closer to Winchester and the Union signal station at Kernstown was dismantled and moved to the outskirts of Winchester.[395]

While the town's Confederate sympathizers scrounged for food and supplies and their Union counterparts provided none, the reopened Winchester and Potomac Railroad carried supplies from Harpers Ferry to Sheridan's army and the winter season for Union

---

[394] Stephen Z. Starr, ed., "Winter Quarters Near Winchester, 1864 - 1865: Reminiscences of Roger Hannaford, Second Ohio Volunteer Cavalry", *Virginia Magazine of History and Biography* 86, no. 3, 322.

[395] Oscar Ireland, Diary Dec. 1, 1864 - Dec. 15, 1865 (Signal Corps), 1180 WFCHS, Handley Archives, entry for December 14, 1864. J. Willard Brown, *The Signal Corps In The War Of The Rebellion* (Baltimore: Butternut and Blue, 1996), 637.

Winchester was soon filled with gala affairs. The final weeks of 1864 and opening weeks of the New Year witnessed numerous social gatherings in town that were attended by Union officers and some of the most prominent Unionist women in town.

During one of these affairs Hattie Griffith, a Unionist who had endured the war, met Captain William Irving Ellis. Ellis, a member of General Sheridan's staff, frequented the parties in town and was introduced to Hattie at one of them. Because the weather was terrible, the two spent much time getting acquainted. Ellis appeared to enjoy life during the winter lull in fighting as Hattie recorded that on January 4, "Captain Ellis called, he was sleighing all day though it was not at all good—just a cracker box...."[396] When Ellis was away from Winchester they corresponded and maintained a strong long-distance relationship for the remainder of the war. Ellis and Hattie later wed in Winchester at the Episcopal Church on October 10, 1865.[397]

Happy times continued among the soldiers and Unionists despite the terrible weather. Sheridan wanted safe passage for his men and civilians on the sidewalks and ordered all walkways be cleared of snow and ice. Many of the town's citizens obeyed Sheridan's order, but some refused, among them Mrs. Lee. In her characteristically rebellious manner, Mrs. Lee sternly refused to clean her walkway of ice, writing on January 2:

---

[396] Griffith, diary entry for January 4, 1865.
[397] Ibid., diary entry for January 4, 1865.

> As Sheridan's order with regard to cleaning the pavements had been obeyed, the walking was very good. I was one of the few contumacious ones & it was merely because I did not choose to obey orders, that I made no effort to have ours cleaned.[398]

As the winter intensified, the last reminder of the short 1864 Valley Campaign, the huge Union field hospital, was broken up on January 3, and Sheridan's final troop deployment to Petersburg was completed on January 6, when his last division—Second Division, XIX Corps—departed from its camp north of town.[399] Sheridan now had only a single infantry division at his disposal, but more than 10,000 cavalry were still available for his use.[400]

On January 23, General William Forsythe, Sheridan's chief of staff, issued an order to General Alfred Torbert, chief of cavalry, concerning the sale of produce. Hattie Griffith, with her inside knowledge of Sheridan's staff, described the nature of the order in her diary.

On Jan. 23 General Forsythe, chief of staff, sent a note to General Torbert, chief of cavalry, to instruct Colonel [Alexander] Pennington, commanding the 3rd Cav. Division, "to permit citizens who have country produce for sale to pass through your lines to Winchester, [they] can obtain the necessary passes given by Col.

---

[398] Lee, diary entry for January 2, 1865.

[399] Griffith, diary entry for January 3, 1865. The entry reads: "The Sheridan Hospital has been broken up entirely."

[400] Delauter, 87.

[Oliver] Edwards to bring in marketing... The marketing is brought in for the citizens and officers of Winchester.[401]

Sheridan decided in early February 1865 to go after another Rebel partisan commander, Harry Gilmor. Gilmor's Maryland cavalry and the local guerrillas under his command might easily hamper Union operations in the spring. Sheridan was aware of the havoc Gilmor created in the region earlier in the war. For example, Gilmor's February 1864 raid on the Baltimore and Ohio Railroad between Duffield's Depot and Kearneysville created such an outcry in Union newspapers that General Lee was forced to have Gilmor tried by court martial. After a one-week trial, Gilmor was exonerated of robbery charges and returned to duty.[402]

Gilmor's reputation and Sheridan's knowledge that by late December 1864 Gilmor had two local partisan companies attached to his cavalry command—McNeill's Rangers and Captain Charles H. Woodson's companies—drove him to end Gilmor's operations. Gilmor inherited McNeill's partisan rangers after their commander died on November 10, 1864, as a result of wounds received on October 2, 1864, at Meem's Bottom.[403]

---

[401] Griffith, diary entry for January 24, 1865.

[402] Gilmor, 146. For a complete biographical study of Gilmor see: Timothy Ackinclose, *Sabres and Pistols: The Civil War Carrer of Colonel Harry Gilmor, C.S.A.* (Gettysburg, Pa.: Stan Clark Military Books, 1997).

[403] Roger U. Delauter, Jr., *McNeill's Rangers* (Lynchburg, Va.: H.E. Howard, 1986), 79-84. These pages discuss the attack at Meem's Bottom and the final weeks of McNeill's life.

Sheridan sent 300 cavalry preceded by Major Henry K. Young, leader of Sheridan's Jessie Scouts, to capture Gilmor.[404] Early on February 4, Young and five men entered the home in Moorefield, West Virginia, where Gilmor was quartered. Gilmor knew them to be Jessie Scouts, but was unable to flee and surrendered.[405]

The captured Gilmor arrived in Winchester around noon on February 5, and was put into a hotel room guarded by two Union soldiers.[406] The empty hotel room had a chalk line drawn on the floor. The line was a "dead line" and if Gilmor crossed it his guards had orders to shoot him. As if this was not enough to keep the slippery Gilmor secured, Sheridan ordered the provost to handcuff his hands and feet.[407] Sheridan allowed only minimal rations for Gilmor and if it were not for the kindness of the lieutenant of the guard, who gave Gilmor two blankets, he might have frozen to death.[408] After three days captivity, Gilmor was escorted by Major Young to Harpers Ferry on the Winchester and Potomac Railroad. By February 10, Gilmor was in Fort Warren Prison in Boston Harbor.[409]

Gilmor's capture angered the other partisans in the Valley and, in retaliation, McNeill's Rangers rode into Cumberland,

---

[404] Gilmor, 277.
[405] Ibid., 277-78.
[406] Ibid., 283.
[407] Driver, 190.
[408] Gilmor, 283.
[409] Ibid., 286.

Maryland, at 3 a.m. on February 21, and captured both Generals George Crook and Benjamin Kelley.[410]   The stealthy rangers evaded Union horsemen who pursued them and took the two generals into captivity. Both officers were later exchanged.[411]

Sheridan fumed over the capture of the generals and took his frustrations out on the secessionist women of Winchester. Mrs. Lee and her family had fallen victim to one of Sheridan's harsh proclamations on February 23, when a Federal soldier told her that when the weather broke she and her family had to leave Winchester.[412] Mrs. Lee visited Sheridan to ask the reason for her family's exile. Sheridan wanted no words with the rebellious Lee and dismissed her from his office. While Mrs. Lee had never met Sheridan before, her presumptions about his rudeness were confirmed – as far as she was concerned.

The weather cleared on February 25, and the fiery woman was loaded into the wagon carrying her possessions and sent south through Confederate lines. Other women had fallen victim to Sheridan's orders and were added to the caravan of exiles. Among them were the daughters of Judge Joseph Sherrard.[413] Mrs. Lee, although defeated, kept a stiff upper lip in her final days at Winchester. She recounted those days at Newtown during the first night of her exile:

---

[410] Sheridan, 127.

[411] Faust, ed., 410.

[412] Lee, diary entry for February 23, 1865.

[413] Delauter, 89.

After staying awake the few hours I was in bed Thursday night [February 23], I made quite an early rise & from the time I was dressed to late at somewhat injudicious as it prevented my attending to the thousand things necessary to be done in breaking up a home in a day. Such kindness I never saw... Mrs. Custer (the General's wife) appealed to Sheridan to send us to our lines, but he said it was too far & promised to send us to Middletown, but of that anon. Our friends came in looking as if they were coming to a funeral & could not understand our not looking gloomy. Many tears were shed, but not by us. Even strong men wept... I hear all sorts of persons were going to the Yankees to make appeals... The officer of our escort came to hurry me, but I told him I would not go until nine – the hour Sheridan had appointed. And such a scene; friends crying; the servants, not only our own, but old attachees of the family weeping bitterly. We

laughed and talked all sorts of Rebel talk & the Yankees gazed in astonishment at seeing people turned out of their homes & not depressed by it. Many of our friends followed us in procession down to Mr. Sherrard's... The whole street was filled with lookers - on: citizens, Yankees, servants - altogether a most motley assemblage. As we rode, being sent out of Sheridan's lines, we felt very independent & said loudly what we pleased. We had two ambulances & an army wagon piled up with baggage; we had an escort of over twenty men...[414]

Mrs. Lee never returned to Winchester and ultimately settled in Baltimore. She died in 1906 and was brought back to rest alongside her husband in the Mount Hebron Cemetery.

---

[414] Lee, diary entry for February 25, 1865.

No Confederate sympathizer in Winchester was safe from Sheridan and their hopes of Early making a counterattack were virtually forgotten. By the end of February, Early had only a token force under his command. Two infantry brigades under the command of Brigadier General Gabriel Wharton remained at Staunton while the rest of Early's command, except Brigadier General John Echols' brigade in southwestern Virginia, was sent to reinforce Lee at Petersburg.

Grant ordered Sheridan to move south, destroy the Virginia Central Railroad, the James River canal, and to secure Lynchburg if possible. Afterward, Sheridan was to link up with General William T. Sherman in North Carolina. Grant gave Sheridan a large amount of discretion and after Sheridan reached Lynchburg and found it impracticable to join Sherman, he completed the destruction of the railroad and canal and then joined Grant near Petersburg.[415] As a result of Sheridan's movements, Grant placed Major General Winfield Scott Hancock in command of the Middle Military Division on February 26, with headquarters at Winchester.[416] Hancock, the former commander of the II Corps, had distinguished himself on many battlefields and now proved an ideal Union commander for Winchester near the war's end because he was sympathetic to the civilians' plight.

---

[415] Sheridan, 345-99. All of the information in the paragraph to this point concerning Sheridan's movements in the early part of 1865 is derived from his memoir.

[416] Glenn Tucker, *Hancock the Superb* (Dayton: Morningside, 1980), 266.

Sheridan departed Winchester on February 27, with two divisions of cavalry.[417] While Jubal Early had little combat capability left, he dispatched Brigadier General Thomas Rosser's cavalry in an attempt to stall Sheridan's cavalry. Union troopers easily ran through Rosser's force near Mount Crawford on March 1.[418] Still, Early kept trying to strike at Sheridan. He mustered as many men as he could, approximately 2,000, and formed them in defensive positions west of Waynesboro.[419] Sheridan's two cavalry divisions crushed "Old Jube" with ease, and to make matters worse, approximately 1,000 of Early's small command was captured.[420]

Sheridan's victory over Early at Waynesboro ended fighting in the Shenandoah Valley. After the battle, Sheridan's cavalry destroyed the railroad from Charlottesville to Lynchburg and moved east for the final month of the Civil War in Virginia.[421] Because the Confederates were no longer a threat in the Valley, except the small nuisance groups of partisans, General Hancock remained at Winchester with one infantry division.

Hancock spent his time in Winchester organizing the Federal forces for action in the Shenandoah Valley, but the

---

[417] George Baylor, *Bull Run to Bull Run: or Four Years in the Army of Northern Virginia* (Washington D.C.: Zenger Publishing Co., 1983), 303.

[418] Stackpole, 385 - 386.

[419] Ibid., 386.

[420] Baylor, 303.

[421] Sheridan, 347.

campaign he prepared for was not needed. The nightmare of war ended for Virginia on Palm Sunday, April 9, 1865, when General Grant accepted the surrender of General Robert E. Lee in the small town of Appomattox Court House.

A native of Pennsylvania, Major General Winfield Scott Hancock graduated eighteenth in the West Point class of 1844. He fought ably in all the campaigns of the Army of the Potomac, but is most recognized for his actions as the commander of the II Corps at the Battle of Gettysburg. He was wounded at Gettysburg and spent the next half year convalescing. Although he returned to the Army of the Potomac to fight in Grant's 1864 Virginia Campaign health problems forced him back to Washington D.C. While recuperating he was put in charge of organizing the Veteran Reserve Corps. Hancock was the ideal Union commander to arrive in town so close to the war's end as he sympathized with Winchester's civilians. After the Civil War he remained in the army. In 1880 he ran for president on the democratic ticket, losing to James Garfield. He died in 1886. (Handley Regional Library)

The citizens of pre-war Winchester could not have foreseen the importance of their town in the cataclysmic war for Confederate independence that most of them supported. The country was now united again but deep wounds needed mending.

The plague of war was concluded and rebuilding began. The process, however, would not be without additional pain for the nation.

The dream of an independent South was now a tragic memory as half of the nation was under Federal military occupation. Winchester was fortunate, however, to be under Hancock's command. Unlike his predecessors, Hancock was no tyrant and did everything possible to ease the burden of his fellow countrymen.[422]

The day after Lee's surrender, Hancock addressed the citizens of Winchester and explained his magnanimous policies.[423] Hancock saw no point in the humiliation and retribution the Radical Republicans planned to impose and kept his promise of no military restraints. He even petitioned the War Department to have some of his troops withdrawn to Harpers Ferry, but his plea fell on deaf ears.[424]

While townspeople began to rebuild their lives, Hancock had to deal with some business left over from the war. Partisans plagued the area in the final months of the Civil War and Mosby and his men were still on the loose. Hancock requested the surrender of Mosby's Rangers, but Mosby had no official

---

[422] For a complete history of Reconstruction in the South refer to: Eric Foner, *Reconstruction: America's Unfinished Revolution, 1863 - 1877* (New York: Perennial Classics, 1988).
[423] Tucker, 266.
[424] *O.R.,* Ser. I, Vol. XLVI, part 3, 714.

correspondence from his superiors and felt he was not authorized to surrender. Mosby did, however, agree to cease attacks until Lee's surrender could be verified.[425]

Hancock met with Mosby's representatives after Lee's surrender was verified. Dr. A. Monteiro, Mosby's surgeon, and three other partisans met with Hancock to discuss the surrender terms. The former II Corps commander was receptive and amiable toward the negotiators. He graciously granted them a two-day armistice and extended the armistice at Mosby's request.[426] Mosby never surrendered his men, but later disbanded them at Salem, Virginia, on April 21.[427]

Hancock, jubilant that the war was over, longed for the company of his beautiful wife, Almira. On April 13, Hancock sent word to his wife to join him in Winchester, and the lovely Almira boarded a train in Baltimore for Winchester on the morning of April 14.[428] Mrs. Hancock made it to the Relay House by the time President Lincoln was shot by John Wilkes Booth. Secretary of War Stanton ordered all trains stopped and searched for the assassin. She was stuck on the train for six hours before departing for Winchester.[429] Hancock, unaware of events in Washington, was awakened at 2 a.m. on April 15, and summoned to the

---

[425] Tucker, 267.

[426] Ibid., 267-68.

[427] Salem, Virginia, is located east of Markham, Virginia.

[428] A.R. Hancock, *Reminiscences of Winfield Scott Hancock* (New York: Charles L. Webster & Company, 1887), 106.

[429] Hancock, 107.

capital.[430] The exhausted Almira joined her husband in Winchester just in time to make a return trip to Washington.

At 7:22 a.m. on April 15, the South's hope for a mild reconstruction process vanished with the death of President Lincoln. Radical Republicans in Congress made their policy retribution rather than reconciliation, and their actions included not only vengeance for the war but retaliation over the death of President Lincoln.

Due to Lincoln's assassination, Hancock moved his headquarters from Winchester to Washington, on April 22. General Torbert assumed command in Winchester.[431]

Andrew Johnson became President after Lincoln's death and sought to implement a policy Lincoln would have wanted. President Johnson's policy for rebuilding the South was lenient. The recently seceded states had only to renounce their ordinance of secession, abolish slavery, and ratify the Thirteenth Amendment. Johnson, however, faced stiff opposition from the Radical Republicans in Congress and they soon paralyzed his plan.

Congress refused to recognize the new state governments set up under Johnson's plan and imposed more requirements for reunion, including the Fourteenth Amendment that granted citizenship to former slaves and free blacks. Johnson had no other choice than to uphold the decisions of Congress; by this point,

---

[430] Ibid.

[431] Delauter, 93.

Johnson had no real political power and bills he vetoed were easily overridden by Congress.

Radical Republicans found it troublesome that southern governments sent former Confederate officials to the United States Congress, among them Alexander Stephens, the Vice President of the Confederacy. Under Congress' new measures, the former Confederate states had to rewrite their state constitutions to include the Thirteenth and Fourteenth Amendments for readmission into the Union.

Winchester during Reconstruction was a model town that made every effort possible to move forward with rebuilding lives and property. Various relief associations from Maryland brought food, clothing, and other necessities to help the citizens of the war-torn region rebuild. There was not as much resentment against the Federal government in Winchester as there was in the rest of the former Confederacy.

For example, Captain William McKinley of the 23rd Ohio Volunteer Infantry was inducted into the Hiram Lodge of Winchester as a master mason on May 3, 1865.[432] McKinley fought in the Third Battle of Winchester and was now inducted into a sacred brotherhood by his former enemies.

During Reconstruction, the former Confederate states had approximately 200,000 Federal troops occupying them to maintain

---

[432] William Mosely Brown, *Freemasonry in Winchester, Virginia* (Staunton, Va.: 1949), 102.

order, but Winchester had no more than 500 soldiers on occupation duty.[433] While Union soldiers in Winchester went about their daily duties, the civilians rebuilt and some began discussing the idea of building a Confederate cemetery. Led by the wife of Philip Williams, the civilians of Winchester did not want the memory of the brave men who fought for the Confederacy to fade. Mrs. Williams, the Ladies Memorial Association, and other citizens worked diligently to purchase five acres of land adjacent to the Mount Hebron Cemetery and relocate the remains of over 3,000 Confederate soldiers to the new memorial cemetery.[434] Financial contributions to get the project underway came from all over the South. The state of Alabama, which lost so many of her sons in the Shenandoah Valley, began the process by contributing $1200.[435]

Eleven months later, on June 6, 1866, the cemetery neared completion and the first Confederate Memorial Day was observed. The date was chosen in remembrance of the day Turner Ashby was killed near Harrisonburg in 1862. Thousands of onlookers listened

---

[433] Richard W. Murphy, et. al., *The Nation Reunited: War's Aftermath* (Alexandria, Va.: Time Life Books, 1987), 61. According to the book no post had more than 500 men during Reconstruction. Richmond and New Orleans were the exception to this rule.

[434] Brandon H. Beck & Charles S. Grunder, *The Three Battles Of Winchester: A History and Guided Tour* (Berryville, Va.: The Civil War Foundation, 1997), 36; Delauter, 94.

[435] Beck & Grunder, *The Three Battles of Winchester: A History and Guided Tour*, 36.

as speeches were given by gentlemen who not so long ago fought on the fields of Winchester. The list of speakers included one of Stonewall Jackson's former staff members, Henry Kyd Douglas and F.W.M. Holliday, a former colonel of the 33rd Virginia Infantry, former Confederate Congressman, and future governor of Virginia.

Federal Reconstruction policies were carried out in the area while the locals honored those who sacrificed their lives for the Confederacy. United States forces in Winchester were most respectful to their fallen foes, and on October 25, 1866, Turner Ashby's remains were brought from Charlottesville to Winchester. A further example of the respect displayed by the U.S. military toward the townspeople occurred when, Captain Brown, commander of the garrison, ordered the Federal flag in the incomplete National Cemetery across the street lowered to half staff.[436]

Confederate Memorial Day continues to be observed in Winchester. The ceremony held in 1889 heard an oration by General Jubal Early. Early had not returned to Winchester since his defeat in 1864, but he now stood on the ground where Generals Ramseur and Grimes saved his command from total annihilation. In his speech at the Stonewall Cemetery, Early recounted his defeat at Winchester and the undaunted courage of the Confederate soldiers. Before General Early closed he thanked the women of

---

[436] Delauter, 95.

Winchester and the Shenandoah Valley for their courage and undying devotion to the Confederacy.[437]

Small incidents of violence occurred from April 1865 until the end of the Union occupation in the Lower Shenandoah Valley in 1870. However, the region was quite calm compared to the rest of the South. Throughout much of the South during Military Reconstruction there was rampant misconduct of Union troops toward civilians and a great deal of disorder. The burning of Brenham, Texas, in September 1866 serves as one of many examples of misconduct by Union soldiers. On one Friday night in September 1866, several Union soldiers chased a black man into a ball being held for whites. The Union soldiers chased the man until they encountered several white men, who fearing for the safety of their wives shot one of the Union soldiers. As a result the Union soldiers set the town ablaze.[438]

Winchester's civilians and Federal occupiers got along in a manner markedly different from the war years. The exception to this environment in October 1868 when General Robert Milroy, one of the most despised Yankees to serve in Winchester returned to town to do some politicking.[439] Milroy tried to give a speech at

---

[437] *Winchester Times*, Wednesday June 12, 1889.

[438] James E. Sefton, *The United States Army and Reconstruction: 1865-1867* (Baton Rouge: Louisiana State University, 1967), 95. More information on the burning of Brenham, Texas and other acts of Union misconduct can be found in this book.

[439] Frederic Morton, *The Story of Winchester in Virginia: The Oldest Town in the Shenandoah Valley* (Strasburg, Va.: Shenandoah Publishing House, 1925), 186-187.

the courthouse, but the onlookers, still full of hatred for him, jeered at him until he withdrew.

Winchester endured only five years of post-war occupation, but several other areas of the South were not as fortunate. Louisiana, South Carolina, and Florida endured seven additional years of harsh Union occupation. Military Reconstruction concluded in the South with the election of Rutherford B. Hayes to the presidency. Hayes, who fought at Winchester in 1864, now held the power to withdraw the remainder of Union troops from the last three states still under military occupation.

A great deal of political maneuvering was done for Hayes to get into the White House. Since there were twenty disputed electoral votes, the election remained undecided and went to the House of Representatives for a final vote. Although Hayes was a Republican, the Democrats agreed to give the disputed votes to him if he would order the withdrawal of the remaining Federal troops from the former seceded states. He agreed, won the election, and ended Military Reconstruction in the South.

Winchester recovered during the post-war years and was visited frequently by Union and Confederate veterans. Union veterans, except for Milroy, were treated politely by townspeople who once hated them. Winchester's civilians had survived the plague of war that struck them so very hard for four years.

Winchester, a Guided Tour

As the primary focus of this book is on the civilian experience during the Civil War, the tour will focus on points of interest within the town itself. Many of the Winchester battle sites have fallen victim to development and only those sites that are easily accessible and in some way maintain their historical appearance are included in this tour. For a complete reference to specific positions during the Winchester battles refer to *The Three Battles of Winchester: A History and Guided Tour*, by Brandon H. Beck and Charles S. Grunder.

Some of the sites on this tour are private property. Before exploring closely make sure that you obtain permission from the owner or overseer.

Enjoy your tour.

To get to your first stop get on Pleasant Valley Avenue and drive north. If you follow the signs to the Old Town Welcome Center you'll be on track. Drive on Pleasant Valley until you come to Cork Street. Turn left at the traffic light. After you turn you will see the Mount Hebron Cemetery on your right. Continue on Cork Street until you come to East Lane and turn right. Note, East Lane is located just before the railroad crossing. On your right you will see the entrance to the Mount Hebron Cemetery. Turn right and follow the road into the cemetery. Drive into the cemetery for several hundred yards. On your left you will see the Stonewall Cemetery, the first stop on the tour.

Stop #1 - Mount Hebron Cemetery/Stonewall Cemetery: There are close to 4,000 Confederate soldiers buried in the Stonewall Cemetery and graves of prominent Confederate officers including, General Turner Ashby, Col. George S. Patton, General Robert Johnston, General Archibald Godwin and others are here. The cemetery is maintained through the assistance of the Turner Ashby Chapter of the United Daughters of the Confederacy.

Memorial to the Ashby Brothers (photo by author)

During the Third Battle of Winchester Generals Ramseur and Grimes fought a rearguard action along a defensive line that ran through the Mount Hebron Cemetery.

To get to the next stop, the National Cemetery, wind your

way out of the cemetery and after making a left on to East Lane, you will be moving parallel with the railroad tracks on your left.

At the "T" intersection, turn left on to Cork Street and go straight until you come to the traffic light at Pleasant Valley Avenue. Turn left on Pleasant Valley. Remain in the left lane and drive until you see the sign for National Avenue (this will be at the first traffic light you come to after you turn on Pleasant Valley). Turn left on National Avenue. Drive several blocks and the cemetery entrance will be on your left.

Stop # 2 - The National Cemetery: As you enter the cemetery you will notice an array of monuments dedicated to various regiments and states. One particular item of interest is the Pennsylvania section, grave number 1022, where rests Amos Suppinger, the first man from Pennsylvania to die in Civil War battle. Suppinger was shot on July 2, 1861, at the Battle of Falling Waters. Suppinger was from Danville, Pennsylvania, and was a member of the 11th Regiment Pennsylvania Volunteer Infantry. Suppinger's last name does not appear correctly on the headstone that it reads "Sappington".

To go to the next stop, drive on National Avenue until you come to East Lane and turn left on to East Lane. Go on East Lane and take a right on to Boscawen Street. Drive on Boscawen until you come to Cameron Street. Turn right on Cameron. Turn very quickly to the right into the public parking lot at the judicial center.

The next part of your tour is a walking tour. Portions of it can be driven, however, with one-way streets and scarce parking it might be difficult (you are strongly encouraged to walk). You will see the Kurtz Center/Visitors Center on your right as you pull in the parking area. This is your next stop.

Stop #3 - The Kurtz Center: This is the visitor's center for Winchester. Inside you will find an assortment of items pertaining to Winchester and Shenandoah Valley History. Here is your point of departure for the walking tour.

As you leave the visitors center turn right and walk up Cameron Street. Cross the street at the traffic light and walk to the Old Town Walking Mall. You will walk between city hall and a bank.

Stop #4 - The Old Court House: Once you are on the walking mall you will immediately notice the Court House to your left. In front of the building stands a Confederate monument that was dedicated in 1916. The steps of the building were used for speeches prior to secession and during the war the structure was used as a hospital for the wounded. In the yard in front and during the war, there was a large fenced in area used as a holding area for prisoners of war from each side. Judge Richard Parker, the judge presiding over the John Brown trial sat on the bench here for several years.

From the Court House walk towards Boscawen Street, if you are facing the Courthouse Boscawen Street will be to your right. You can use your map to orient yourself. Cross Boscawen Street and move into the next block of the walking mall. As you walk you will come to a large brick church on your left. This is the Loudoun Street Presbyterian Church, your next stop.

Stop # 5 - The Loudoun Street Presbyterian Church: It is here that the Reverend Andrew H. H. Boyd preached. Boyd was dedicated to the cause of the Confederacy and later arrested by Union soldiers for those convictions. Boyd often mixed politics with his sermons from the pulpit and Diarist Julia Chase recorded Boyd's tendency to preach politics: "Dr. Boyd preached today. I think if he would dispense with politics in the pulpit, it would be better for the community."[440] Officers on both sides attended services here and the church served as a hospital during the war.

To continue on to your next stop, go back to the courthouse, continue on past it until you arrive at a large three story blue structure. This is the Taylor Hotel.

Stop #6 - The Taylor Hotel: Stonewall Jackson spent several days here in November, 1861 before moving his headquarters to the Moore home. Other officers, including Union General Sigel, used the building as quarters. Turner Ashby was promoted to brigadier general on May 27, 1862 in this building.

Your next stop is the Philip Williams' House. Walk up the

---

[440] Chase, diary entry for August 22, 1861.

mall until you come Picadilly Street. When you get to Picadilly Street, there will be two banks to your front. Turn left on Picadilly Street. As you walk on Picadilly Street you will come to Indian Alley. Cross Indian Alley.

Stop #7 - The Philip Williams' House: The Philip Williams' House has heavy wrought iron railings and is the house where Colonel George S. Patton died on September 25, 1864. Patton was the grandfather of General George S. Patton of World War II fame.

Continue to walk on Picadilly Street until you come to the intersection of Picadilly and Braddock Streets. On the corner is your next stop, the Logan home.

Stop #8 - The Logan Home: The large white building with the huge apple monument in front is the Logan family home. The Logans were exiled from their home in 1863 by General Milroy and their home was used by other officers throughout the Union occupations. General Philip Sheridan also used this house as his headquarters after defeating General Early in the 1864 Shenandoah Valley Campaign.

You must drive to the next stop, Stonewall Jackson's headquarters, so go way back to the parking area. From the parking lot, turn right on Cameron Street and get into the left lane. As you drive on Cameron Street, the area between the police station and the George Washington Hotel was once the location of the home of Mrs. Lee. Drive on Cameron until you come to Picadilly Street, turn left and get into the right lane. Drive straight on Picadilly and after the third traffic light, the road will curve to the right to become Fairmont Avenue. Drive north on Fairmont Avenue until you come to North Avenue and turn right. Drive down North Avenue until you come to Braddock Street and turn right. Continue on Braddock Street and make sure you are in the right lane. On the right you will see signs for Stonewall Jackson's Headquarters Museum.

Stop #9 - Stonewall Jackson's Headquarters: 415 North Braddock Street. The home was built in 1854 by Dr. Fuller, a Winchester dentist. In 1856, Fuller sold the home to Lewis Tilghman Moore a Winchester attorney and militia colonel. This is the building where Stonewall Jackson set up his headquarters in early November 1861. Jackson, after his Romney Campaign, returned to Winchester but made his residence down the street at the home of Reverend Graham while continuing to use this building as his office while he resided with the Grahams. Jackson left this building on March 11, 1862, as he was pressured by the approach of General Banks. The museum is operated by the Winchester-Frederick County Historical Society and is open for guided tours.

After completing your tour of Jackson's Headquarters, drive down Braddock Street to the next block. This will take you to the next stop, the Presbyterian Manse, 319 North Braddock Street.

Stop #10 - The Presbyterian Manse: 319 North Braddock Street, Please note that this is now a private residence. This was the home of the Reverend and Mrs. Graham. Reverend Graham was the minister at the Kent Street Presbyterian Church and Mrs. Jackson stayed with the Grahams while her husband was on the Romney Campaign. When Jackson returned in late January he also resided with the Grahams.

To continue on to your next stop, drive down Braddock Street until you come to the intersection of Amherst and Braddock Strects. The corner is your next stop.

Stop #11 - The Boyhood Home of Dr. Hunter McGuire: 103 Braddock Street. The building is currently used as a law office. This is the boyhood home of Dr. McGuire, Stonewall Jackson's physician and medical director. Stonewall Jackson dined in this house with McGuire's parents in late October 1862.

Drive down Braddock Street until you come to Cork Street and make a right. Continue on Cork until you come to Stewart Street, make a right, and continue on Stewart until you arrive at Boscawen Street. You will be at a traffic light when you come to the intersection of Boscawen and Stewart. As you are stopped at the traffic light; notice the dark red brick home to your front left, the next stop on your tour. Please note that on the tour map the Seevers' home appears on the right side of Stewart Street, but the stop number had to be placed there due to the inset map. The home is privately owned and it is not the easiest location to find parking.

Stop #12 - The Seevers' Home: Corner of Stewart and Braddock Streets. This dark red brick building was used by General Banks in 1862. General Shields also used the Seevers' home to convalesce after being wounded by artillery fragments at Kernstown on March 22, 1862.

Continue on to your next stop by turning left at the traffic light and on to Boscawen Street. Boscawen Street curves and runs into Amherst Street. Continue on Amherst Street until you arrive at Hawthorne Drive. Turn right on to Hawthorne Drive. (Note: if you pass the hospital you have gone too far.) As you continue up Hawthorne Drive there is a small hill to your left. There is a large house visible through the trees. This is your stop. You can park on the road.

Stop #13 - Hawthorn: This home is currently a private residence and you cannot approach the property closer. You may go to the stone wall to catch a glimpse of the home.

During the war, this home was owned by Angus McDonald. His wife was Cornelia McDonald, one of the women who kept a detailed record of the war in Winchester.

Continue to your next stop by driving up Hawthorne Drive several hundred yards until you arrive at a circle where you can turn around. Proceed down Hawthorne Drive until you arrive at Amherst Street and turn left. Be careful for traffic coming from your right. As you retrace your route from the Seevers' house, the road will bend back and Amherst Street will become Boscawen Street. Continue straight on Boscawen Street past the Seevers' House until you are at Cameron Street. Turn left and stay in the right lane. Drive north on Cameron and follow the signs to Route 11 North. Drive north on Cameron street until you come to a "Y". Turn right at the "Y", and you will be on Route 11 North. Continue straight until you come to the first traffic light. There is a right turn lane at this point. Turn right on to route 783, cross the railroad tracks, and immediately take a left on to Brick Kiln Road. This will take you to your next stop.

Stop #14 - Fort Collier: Currently the property is under private ownership, but it is possible to gain access to the property with permission from the current renters. The property is currently under contract to be purchased as a educational center. If the current occupiers grant you permission to enter, part of the earthworks are located in the front of the house.

It is here that the decisive Union cavalry charge smashed into Early's left flank during the Third Battle of Winchester. If you face north, this is the direction from which the Union cavalry approached the fortification. Colonel George S. Patton's Brigade was positioned in the west end of the fort.

Continue to your next stop by returning to Route 11, continue north, i.e. turn right and drive north for several miles. Go underneath Interstate 81 and a battlefield marker will be located on your left side. This marks the site of Rutherford's Farm, the location of Ramseur's defeat in July 1864. At Route 761, Old Charlestown Road, turn right. After a short distance you will cross over a bridge. Shortly afterwards Milburn Road will be on your right, turn right on to Milburn Road. After several hundred yards, there will be a battlefield marker. A small parking area is available here.

Stop #15 - Stephenson's Depot: This is the only site common to all three battles. Stonewall Jackson's men lined the lane after the First Battle of Winchester and separated as the General rode down it. During Second Winchester, this is the site of Milroy's decisive defeat. The bridge you crossed is in the location of the bridge used during the Second Battle of Winchester. This was the center of the Confederate line that was held by two of Snowden Andrews' guns. At Third Winchester Union Cavalry probed all morning at the Confederate lines and used this ground as the staging area for the grand cavalry assault on Fort Collier.

The route to your next stop requires driving straight on

Milburn Road. This is a gravel road so drive slowly. Beautiful scenery will surround you as you drive through and Milburn Cemetery will be on your left. There are some graves dating back to colonial times. Continue on Milburn Road until you come to Redbud Road at a "T" intersection. Turn right and follow the road until you see the APCWS sign for the Third Battle of Winchester on the left. There is a large paved parking area here.

Stop #16 - Third Winchester/Hackwood: This is the site of the VIII Corps action during Third Winchester. The property was purchased by APCWS and can be explored with permission from the Civil War Preservation Trust. After obtaining permission to explore the fields, follow the tree line down to Red Bud Run. There is a wooden bridge over it. The narrow road to the right of the parking area goes to Hackwood. Hackwood was built in 1777 and was destroyed during the Civil War. The home is now privately owned. If you wish to explore, check with the owners first.

You can orient yourself by using the Third Winchester map provided in the book. The VIII Corps advanced to strike Early's left moving towards Hackwood, and across Red Bud Run (or away from you if you are standing in the parking area).

After you are done at this site, turn left and continue on Redbud Road until you arrive at Route 11. Right will take you north, left will take you back to Winchester, following 11 South will take you to Interstate 81 North.

This concludes your tour.

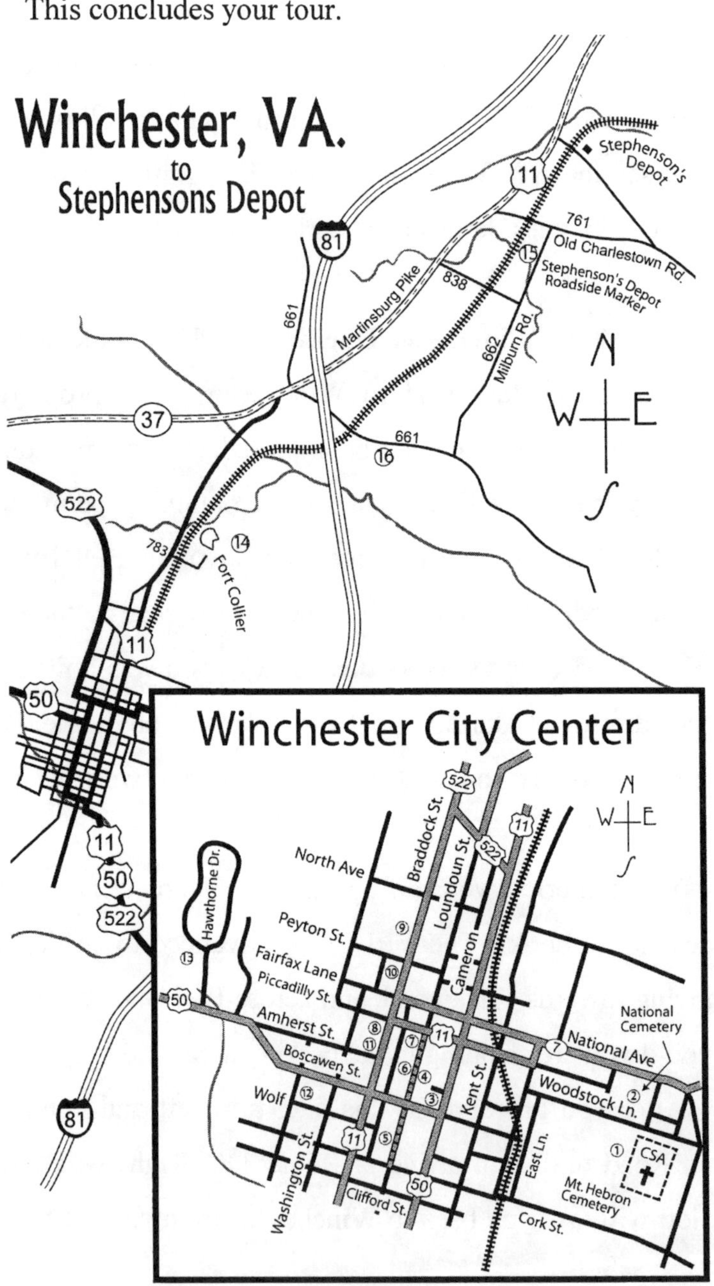

Manuscript Collections

Baker, Portia Baldwin, "Diary, Sept. 19, 1859 - Jan. 8, 1863" 1178 WFCHS, Archives Room, Handley Regional Library, Winchester, VA.

Barritt, Charles M. "Diary, January 1, 1864 - November 10, 1864" 208 WFCHS – Allan Tischler Collection, Archives Room, Handley Regional Library, Winchester, VA.

Brooke, Rev. Benjamin F., "Journal, Sept. 1837 - Dec. 25. 1863" 165 WFCHS – Brooke Collection, Archives Room, Handley Regional Library, Winchester, VA.

Chase, Julia, "War - Time Diary of Miss Julia Chase, 1861 -1 1864" [typescript]. Archives Room, Handley Regional Library, Winchester,VA.

Clark, John Peyton, "Journal, March 12, 1862 - Sept. 15, 1862" 424 WFCHS – Lousia Crawford Collection, Archives Room, Handley Regional Library, Winchester, VA.

Grabill, John H. "Diary, June 6, 1861 - June 6, 1862" 36 WFCHS - Charles Affleck Collection, Archives Room, Handley Regional Library, Winchester, VA.

Griffith, Harriet H., "Diary, April 18, 1861 - Dec. 26, 1865" 1179 WFCHS – Harriet Hollingsworth Griffith Collection, Archives Room, Handley Regional Library, Winchester, VA.

Ireland, Oscar, "Diary, Dec. 1, 1864 - Dec. 15, 1865" 1180 WFCHS, Archives Room, Handley Regional Library, Winchester, VA.

Jones, Maj. Frank B., "Diary, March 11, 1862 - November 17, 1865" 424 WFCHS - Lousia Crawford Collection, Archives Room, Handley Regional Library, Winchester, VA.

Selected Bibliography

Lee, Mrs. Hugh, "Diary, March 11, 1862 - November 17, 1865"
1182 WFCHS - Mrs. Hugh Lee Collection, Archives Room,
Handley Regional Library, Winchester, VA.

Miller, Gettie [Margaretta], "Diary, March 23, 1863 - Sept. 9,
1863" 301 WFCHS - Godfrey Miller Collection, Archives Room,
Handley Regional Library. Winchester, VA.

Sperry, Kate, "Diary, Surrender? Never Surrender, July 13 - 1861 -
Dec. 3, 1865" Archives Room, Handley Regional Library,
Winchester, VA.

Tull, William Bayliss. "Memoirs, July, 1862 - Sept., 1864" 15
WFCHS - THL, Archives Room, Handley Regional Library,
Winchester, VA.

Other Archives/Collections Used

Alabama Department of Archives and History, Montgomery,
Alabama.

National Archives and Records Administration. RG 393, Vol. II,
Special Orders. Apr. 1862 – June 1863.

Robert H. Milroy Collection, Jasper County Public Library,
Rensselaer, Indiana.

Published Primary Sources

Battles and Leaders of the Civil War. 4 Vols. Castle, Edison, Nj.

Beck, Brandon H. ed., *Third Alabama! The Civil War Memoir of
Brigadier General Cullen Andrews Battle, CSA.* Tuscaloosa:
University of Alabama Press, 2000

Colt, Margaretta Barton. *Defend the Valley: A Shenandoah Family
in the Civil War.* Oxford: Oxford University Press, 1994.

Selected Bibliography

Douglas, Henry Kyd. *I Rode With Stonewall*. Marietta: Mockingbird Books, 1995

Duncan, Richard R., ed. *Alexander Neil and The Last Shenandoah Valley Campaign: Letter of an Army Surgeon to His Family, 1864.* Shippensburg, Pa.: White Mane Publishing, 1996.

Early, Jubal A. *A Memoir of the Last Year of the War for Independence in the Confederate States of America.* Columbia: University of South Carolina Press, 2001.

__________. *War Memoirs: Autobiographical Sketch and Narrative of the War Between the States: Jubal Anderson Early Lieutenant General, C.S.A.* Bloomington: Indiana University Press, 1960.

Freeman, Dougals Southall, ed., *Lee's Dispatches*. Baton Rouge: Louisiana State University,1994.

Gilmor, Colonel Harry. *Four Years in the Saddle*. New York: Harper & Brothers, 1866.

Grant, U.S. *Personal Memoirs of U.S. Grant.* 2 Vols. New York: Charles L. Webster & Co., 1886.

Gwin, Minrose C., ed. *A Woman's Civil War, A Diary With Reminiscences of the War, From March 1862, Cornelia Peake McDonald.* Madison: The University of Wisconsin Press, 1992.

Hancock, A.R. *Reminiscences of Winfield Scott Hancock.* New York: Charles L. Webster & Company, 1886.

Jackson, Mary Anna. *Memoirs of "Stonewall" Jackson.* Dayton, Oh.: Morningside, 1993

Jones, Terry L., ed. *The Civil War Memoirs of Captain William J. Seymour: Reminiscences of a Louisiana Tiger*. Baton Rouge: Louisiana State University Press, 1991.

Selected Bibliography

McMullen, Glenn L, ed. *A Surgeon with Stonewall Jackson, The Civil War Letters of Dr. Harvey Black.* Baltimore: Butternut & Blue, 1995.

McDonald, Archie P. ed. *Make Me a Map Of The Valley - The Civil War Journal Of Stonewall Jackson's Topographer, Jedediah Hotchkiss.* Dallas: Southern Methodist University Press, 1989.

Orville, Thomson. *From Philippi to Appomattox: Narrative of the Seventh Indiana Infantry in the War for the Union.* Baltimore: Butternut and Blue, 1993.

Paulus, Margaret B. (comp.). *Papers of General Robert Huston Milroy.* 4 Vols. n.p., 1965.

Schmidt, Martin F., ed. *General George Crook: His Autobiography.* Norman: University of Oklahoma Press, 1946.

Sheridan, Philip H. *The Personal Memoirs of P.H. Sheridan.* New York: DaCapo Press, 1992.

U.S. War Department (comp.). *War of the Rebellion: A Compilation of the Official Records of the Union and Confederate Armies.* 128 Vols. Washington: U.S. Government Printing Office, 1880 - 1901

Articles/Newspapers

Blaisdell, Lowell L. "A French Civil War Adventurer: Fact and Fancy." *Civil War History A Journal of the Middle Period.* (XII, 1966), 246-57.

Collins. Cary C., "Grey Eagle: Major General Robert Huston Milroy and the Civil War." *Indiana Magazine of History and Biography* (March 1994): 48-72.

Dannett, Sylvia G. "Rebecca Wright -- Traitor or Patriot?" *Lincoln*

Selected Bibliography

Herald (Fall 1963): 103-12.

Edwards, William B., "Guns For The South." *Confederate Veteran* (I, 2001): 8 - 11.

Feis, William B. "Neutralizing The Valley: The Role of Military Intelligence In The Defeat of Jubal Early's Army of the Valley, 1864 - 1865." *Civil War HistoryA Journal of the Middle Period.* Kent State University Press (September 1993): 199-215.

Geier, Clarence, Warren Hofstra & Joseph Whitehorne. "The Sheridan Military Field Hopital Complex at Shawnee Springs." *Winchester - Frederick County Historical Society Journal* (VII, 1993): 17-32.

Graham, James Robert, "Some Reminiscences of Stonewall Jackson". *Things and Thoughts.* (I, 1901).

Hemingway, Albert, "Whirling Through Winchester." *America's Civil War* (May 1991): 38-44.

Jones, Terry L. "Going Back Into the Union At Last: A Lousiana Tiger's Account of the Gettysburg Campaign." *Civil War Times Illustrated* (Jan./Feb. 1991): 55 - 60.

Kohlbus, Lenora, "Colonel Harry Gilmore, CSA, Maryland Cavalier." *UDC Magazine* (April 2001): 18-19.

Mewborn, Horace, "The Operations of Mosby's Rangers." *Blue & Gray* (Summer 2000): 6-14, 16-21, 40-50.

Moore, James Tice. "Of Cavaliers and Yankees Frederick W.M. Holliday and the Sectional Crisis 1845 - 1861." *Virginia Magazine of History and Biography,* 99 (3): 352-359.

Riggs, David F. "Robert Young Conrad and the Ordeal of Secession." *Virginia Magazine of History and Biography,* 86 (3): 259-274.

Selected Bibliography

Starr, Stephen Z. ed., "Winter Quarters Near Winchester, 1864 - 1865: Reminiscences of Roger Hannaford, Second Ohio Cavalry." *Virginia Magazine of History and Biography,* 86 (3): 320-38.

Wert, Jeffry D. "The Second Battle of Kernstown, 1864." *Civil War Times Illustrated* (October 1984): 40-47.

"Winchester Times". Wednesday, June 12, 1889

Published Sources

Ackinclose, Timothy. *Sabres and Pistols: The Civil War Career of Colonel Harry Gilmor, C.S.A.* Gettysburg, Pa.: Stan Clark Military Books, 1997.

Allen, T.Harrel. *Lee's Last Major General: Bryan Grimes of North Carolina.* Mason City, Ia.: Savas Publishing, 1999.

Allen, William, *History of the Campaign of Gen. T.J. (Stonewall) Jackson in the Shenandoah Valley of Virginia from November 4, 1861 - June 17, 1862.* Dayton, Oh.: Morningside, 1991.

Beach, William H. A.M. *The First New York (Lincoln) Cavalry from April 19, 1861 To July 7, 1865.* Annandale: Bacon Race Books, 1998.

Bean, W.G. *Stonewall's Man: Sandie Pendleton.* Chapel Hill: The University of North Carolina Press, 1959.

Beck, Brandon H. & Charles S. Grunder. *The First Battle of Winchester.* Lynchburg, Va.: H.E. Howard, 1992.

_______________. *The Second Battle of Winchester.* Lynchburg, Va.: H.E. Howard, 1989.

Beck, Brandon H. & Roger U. Delauter. *The Third Battle of Winchester.* Lynchburg, Va: H.E. Howard, 1997.

Beck, Brandon H. & Charles S. Grunder. *The Three Battles of Winchester, a History and Guided Tour.* Berryville, Va.: The Civil War Foundation, 1997.

Brown, Willard J., *The Signal Corps in the War of the Rebellion.* Baltimore: Butternut and Blue, 1996.

Bushong, Millard K. *General Turner Ashby and Stonewall's Valley Campaign.* Waynesboro, Va.: The McClung Corp, 1992.

________. *Old Jube.* Shippensburg, Pa.: White Mane Publishing Company, 1990.

Clark, Champ et. al. *Decoying the Yanks: Jackson's Valley Campaign.* Alexandria: Time Life, 1984.

Cohen, Stan. *John Brown "The Thundering Voice of Jehovah".* Missoula, Mt.: Pictorial Histories, 1999.

Davis, William C. *Breckinridge: Statesman, Soldier, Symbol.* Baton Rouge: Louisiana State University Press, 1974.

____________. *The Battle of New Market.* Baton Rouge: Louisiana State University Press, 1975.

Downer, Edward T. *Stonewall Jackson's Shenandoah Valley Campaign 1862.* Lexington, Va.: Stonewall Jackson Memorial Incorporated, 1959.

Delauter, Roger U., Jr. *McNeill's Rangers.* Lynchburg, Va.: H.E. Howard, 1986.

______________. *Winchester in the Civil War.* Lynchburg, Va.: H.E. Howard, 1992.

.Dreese, Michael A. *The 151st Pennsylvania at Gettysburg: Like Ripe Apples in a Storm.* Jefferson, N.C.: McFarland & Company, 2000.

Selected Bibliography

Driver, Robert J. Jr. *First and Second Maryland Cavalry, C.S.A.* Charlottesville, Va.: Rockbridge Publishing, 1999.

Ecelbarger, Gary L. *"We are in for it!" The First Battle of Kernstown.* Shippensburg, Pa.: White Mane Publishing, 1997.

Faust, Patricia L. ed., *Historical Times Illustrated Encyclopedia of the Civil War.* New York: Harper - Perennial, 1986.

Foner, Eric. *Reconstruction: America's Unfinished Revolution, 1863 - 1877.* New York: Perennial Classics, 1988.

Freeman, Douglas Southall. *R.E. Lee.* 4 Vols. New York: Charles Scribner's Sons, 1934.

_______________________. *Lee's Lieutenants.* 3 Vols. New York:Charles Scribner's Sons, 1942.

Gallagher, Gary W. *Stephen D. Ramseur: Lee's Gallant General.* Chapel Hill: The University of North Carolina Press, 1985.

_______________, ed. *Struggle for the Shenandoah: Essays on the 1864 Valley Campaign.* Kent: The Kent State University Press, 1991.

Harwell, Richard B. *The Union Reader.* Secaucus, N.J.: The Blue and Gray Press, 1958.

Haselberger, Fritz. *Confederate Retaliation: McCausland's 1864 Raid.* Shippensburg, Pa.: Burd Street Press, 2000.

Hassler, William Woods. *Colonel John Pelham, Lee's Boy Artillerist.* Chapel Hill: The University of North Carolina Press, 1960.

Hearn, Chester G. *When the Devil Came Down to Dixie: Ben Butler in New Orleans.* Baton Rouge: Louisiana State University

Press, 1997.

Henderson, G.F.R. *Stonewall Jackson and the American Civil War*. New York: DaCapo, 1943.

Hennessy, John J. *Return to Bull Run: The Campaign and Battle of Second Manassas*. Norman: University of Oklahoma Press, 1993.

Hutton, Paul Andrew. *Phil Sheridan and His Army*. Lincoln: University of Nebraska Press, 1985.

Katz, Philip M. *From Appomattox to Montmartre: Americans and the Paris Commune*. Cambridge: Harvard University Press, 1998.

Krick, Robert K. *Conquering the Valley: Stonewall Jackson at Port Republic*. New York: William Morrow, 1996.

____________. *Lee's Colonels*. Dayton, Oh.: Morningside, 1979.

____________. *Stonewall Jackson at Cedar Mountain*. Chapel Hill: University of North Carolina Press, 1990.

Lehman, Same, ed. *The Story of Frederick County*. 1989.

Lewis, Thomas A. *The Shenandoah in Flames, the Valley Campaign of 1864*. Alexandria: Time Life Books, 1987.

Lowry, Terry D. *22nd Virginia Infantry*. Lynchburg, Va.: H.E. Howard, 1988.

____________. *"To Live and Die in Dixie" How The South Formed A Nation*. Murfreesboro: Southern Heritage Press, 1999.

McPherson, James M., ed. *The Atlas of the Civil War*. New York: Macmillan, 1994.

Selected Bibliography

__________. *Battle Cry of Freedom.* New York: Ballantine Books, 1988.

Miller, Edward A., Jr. *Lincoln's Abolitionist General: The Biography of David Hunter.* Columbia: University of South Carolina Press, 1997.

Morton, Frederic. *The Story of Winchester in Virginia: The Oldest Town in the Shenandoah Valley.* Strasburg, Va.: Shenandoah Publishing House, 1925.

Murphy, Richard W. *The Nation Reunited: War's Aftermath.* Alexandria: Time Life Books, 1987.

Norris, J.E. *History of the Lower Shenandoah Valley Counties of Frederick, Berkeley, Jefferson, and Clarke.* Chicago: A. Warner and Company, 1890.

Northern Virginia Daily. *Standing Ground: The Civil War In The Shenandoah Valley.* Strasburg, Va.: Shenandoah Publishing House, Inc., 1996.

Patton, Robert H. *The Pattons: A Personal History of an American Family.* Washington D.C.: Brassey's,1994.

Perret, Geoffrey. *Ulysses S. Grant: Soldier & President.* New York: Random House, 1997.

Perry, Mark. *Conceived in Liberty: Joshua Chamberlain, William Oates, and the American Civil War.* New York: Penguin Books, 1997.

Pfanz, Donald. *Richard S. Ewell: A Soldier's Life.* Chapel Hill: University of North Carolina Press, 1998.

Philips, Edward H. *The Lower Shenandoah Valley in the Civil War: The Impact of War Upon the Civilian Population and Upon Civilian Institutions.* Lynchburg, Va.: H.E. Howard, 1993.

Quarles, Garland R. *Occupied Winchester, 1861 - 1865.* Winchester, Va: Winchester - Frederick Country Historical Society, 1991.

__________. *The Story of One Hundred Old Homes in Winchester, Virginia.* Winchester, Va.:   Farmers & Merchants National Bank, 1967.

Robertson, James I. Jr. *Stonewall Jackson: The Man, The Soldier, The Legend.* New York: Macmillan, 1997.

__________. *The Stonewall Brigade.* Baton Rouge: Louisiana State University Press, 1991.

Roland, Charles P. *The American Iliad: The Story of the American Civil War.* Boston: McGraw Hill, 1991.

Sauers, Richard A. *The Devastating Hand of War: Romney West Virginia During The Civil War.* Glen Ferris, W.V.: Gauley Mount Press, 2000.

Schildt, John W. *Hunter Holmes McGuire: Doctor in Gray.* Chewsville, Md.: Self published, 1986.

Schmidt, Lewis G. *A Civil War History of the 47th Regiment of Pennsylvania Veteran Volunteers.* Allentown, Pa.: Self published, 1986.

Scott, J.L. *23rd Battalion Virginia Infantry.* Lynchburg, Va.: H.E. Howard, 1991.

__________. *Lowry's, Bryan's and Chapman's Batteries of Virginia Artillery.* Lynchburg, Va.:   H.E. Howard, 1988.

Sears, Stephen W. *To the Gates of Richmond: The Peninsula Campaign.* New York: Ticknor and Fields, 1992.

Sefton, James E. *The United States Army and Reconstruction:*

1865-1867. Baton Rouge: Louisiana State University Press, 1967.

Stackpole, Edward J. *Sheridan in the Shenandoah*. Harrisburg, Pa.: Stackpole Books, 1992.

Stouffer, Cindy & Shirley Cubbison. *A Colonel, A Flag, And A Dog*. Gettysburg, Pa.: Thomas Publications, 1998.

Symonds, Craig L. *Joseph E. Johnston: A Civil War Biography*. New York: W.W. Norton and Company, 1992.

Tanner, Robert G. *Stonewall in the Valley: Thomas J. 'Stonewall' Jackson's Shenandoah Valley Campaign, Spring 1862*. Garden City: Doubleday and Company, Inc., 1976.

Time Life Books, ed. *Voices of the Civil War: Shenandoah 1862*. Alexandria: Time Life Books,1997.

Tucker, Glenn. *Hancock the Superb*. Dayton, Oh.: Morningside, 1980.

Vandiver, Frank E. *Mighty Stonewall: The Life and Campaigns of General Thomas Jackson*. College Station: Texas A & M University Press, 1957.

Wallace, Lee A. Jr., *5th Virginia Infantry*. Lynchburg, Va.: H.E. Howard, 1988.

Wayland, John W. *Twenty-Five Chapters on the Shenandoah Valley: To Which is Appended a Concise History of the Civil War in the Valley*. Harrisonburg, Va.: C.J. Carrier Co., 1976.

Wert, Jeffry D. *From Winchester to Cedar Creek: The Shenandoah Campaign of 1864*. Mechanicsburg, Pa.: Stackpole Books, 1997.

Wittenberg, Eric J. *Glory Enough for All: Sheridan's Second Raid and the Battle of Trevilian Station*. Washington D.C.: Brassey's,

2001.

Boyd, Rev. Dr. Andrew H.H.: Sympathetic to the Confederacy, he was born in Martinsburg, Virginia (presently West Virginia) in 1814. He graduated from Jefferson College, Yale, Princeton Theological Seminary, and the University of Edinburgh. He became pastor of Winchester's Loudoun Street Presbyterian Church in 1842 and remained in that capacity until his death in 1868.

Brooke, Rev. Benjamin F.: He was born in 1820 and ordained in 1843. He came to Winchester in 1860 and served as the pastor of the Market Street Methodist Church until 1863. Although not in favor of secession at first, he supported the cause of the Confederacy once Virginia seceded in 1861. He died in 1882.

Conrad, Robert Y.: He was born in 1805 and educated at West Point, however, he withdrew before graduation. Conrad served as one of the delegates to the Virginia Secession Convention in 1861. He was initially strongly opposed to secession, and voted against it twice. After Virginia seceded he supported his state and sent several of his sons into the Confederate Army.

Chase, Julia: Sympathetic to the Union, she was born in Maine in 1831 and her family later moved to Winchester. She resided with her parents in Winchester during the war in a home situated at the corner of Loudoun Street and Fairfax Lane. She died in 1906 and is buried in Winchester's Mount Hebron Cemetery.

Graham, Rev. Robert: He was born in 1824 and was a strong supporter of the Confederacy. He served as pastor of the Kent Street Presbyterian Church from 1851-1900 and pastor emeritus of the Loudoun Street Presbyterian Church from 1900-1914. He died in 1914. He and his wife Fanny had a close relationship with General Thomas J. "Stonewall" Jackson and wife Mary Anna. Perhaps no Winchester resident knew Jackson more intimately than Rev. Graham.

Lee, Mrs. Mary (Hugh): Born on September 9, 1819, she married Hugh Holmes Lee in 1843. During the war she lived at 132 North Cameron Street and was perhaps one of Winchester's strongest civilian supporters of the Confederacy. After being exiled from Winchester by General Sheridan in 1865, Lee ultimately ended up settling in Baltimore, Maryland. She died in Baltimore in 1907 and was brought to Winchester for burial in the Mount Hebron Cemetery.

McDonald, Cornelia: A staunch supporter of the Confederacy, she was born in Alexandria, Virginia in 1822. She married Angus McDonald in 1847. Her husband later served as a colonel in the Confederate cavalry. Cornelia left Winchester in July 1863 and went to Lexington, Virginia. In 1873 she moved with her son in

Kentucky. She died in 1909. She is buried in the Hollywood Cemetery in Richmond, Virginia alongside her husband, who died in 1864 as a result of his weakened condition from being imprisoned by Union General David Hunter.

Sperry, Kate: She was eighteen years old when the war broke out. Her father Warden Warren Sperry served in the 2nd Virginia Volunteer Infantry. Kate was among Winchester's staunch Confederate supporters. She died in 1886, at the age of forty-three from a heart attack.

Wright, Rebecca: She was twenty-three years old during the first year of the Civil War. As a Quaker School Teacher she was a strong proponent of the Union, and it was her message to General Sheridan in mid-September 1864 that prompted Sheridan to attack General Early at Winchester on September 19, 1864. She died in 1914.

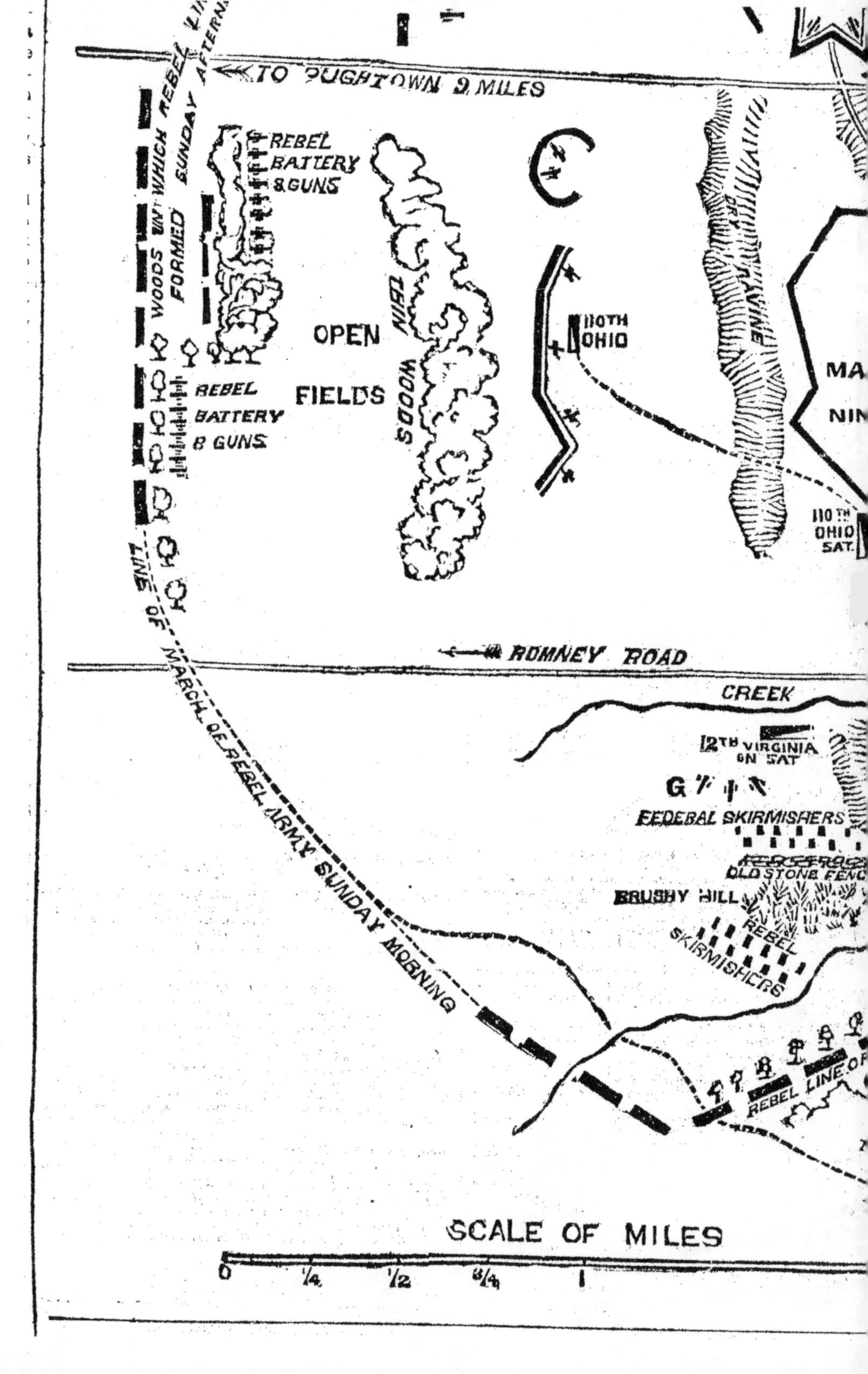

TO PUGHTOWN 9 MILES
WOODS IN WHICH REBEL LINE FORMED SUNDAY AFTERN
LINE OF MARCH OF REBEL ARMY SUNDAY MORNING
REBEL BATTERY 8 GUNS
REBEL BATTERY 8 GUNS
OPEN FIELDS
THIN WOODS
110TH OHIO
110TH OHIO SAT.
DRY RAVINE
MA
NIN
ROMNEY ROAD
CREEK
12TH VIRGINIA ON SAT
G
FEDERAL SKIRMISHERS
OLD STONE FENCE
BRUSHY HILL
REBEL SKIRMISHERS
REBEL LINE OF
SCALE OF MILES
0   1/4   1/2   3/4   1